STUDY GUIDE

THE
SUPERNATURAL
POWER
OF A
TRANSFORMED
MIND

DESTINY IMAGE BOOKS BY BILL JOHNSON

A Life of Miracles

Dreaming With God

Center of the Universe

Momentum

Release the Power of Jesus

Strengthen Yourself in the Lord

The Supernatural Power of a Transformed Mind

Hosting the Presence

THE
SUPERNATURAL
POWER
OF A
TRANSFORMED
MIND

ACCESS TO A LIFE OF MIRACLES

BILL JOHNSON

2/25/17.

DESTINY IMAGE® PUBLISHERS, INC.

P.O. Box 310, Shippensburg, PA 17257-0310

"Promoting Inspired Lives"

This book and all other Destiny Image, Revival Press, MercyPlace, Fresh Bread, Destiny Image Fiction, and Treasure House books are available at Christian bookstores and distributors worldwide.

For a U.S. bookstore nearest you, call 1-800-722-6774.

For more information on foreign distributors, call 717-532-3040.

Reach us on the Internet: www.destinyimage.com.

ISBN 13 TP: 978-0-7684-0423-4

ISBN 13 Ebook: 978-0-7684-0424-1

For Worldwide Distribution, Printed in the U.S.A.

9 10 11 12 13 / 18 17 16

CONTENTS

USING THE STUDY GUIDE

This study guide provides you with interactive sessions that you will go through together as a group. Additionally, you will have five daily reinforcement exercises. This is not intended to give you busywork, adding to what you are already doing. One of the primary steps to experiencing a transformed mind is through biblical meditation. These activities are specifically designed to aid in this process.

In the daily exercises you will engage the questions that follow each of the entries. As you go through each one, yielded to the Holy Spirit's direction and dependent upon His instruction, you will go from "glory to glory" in your relationship with the Lord and will be transformed into a growing disciple who thinks from Heaven's perspective.

Each daily assignment ends with a *Transformation Thought* that summarizes the day's topic; *Reflection Questions* for your interaction; a *Transformation Prayer* that will help you personalize and seal the truth you learned; and finally, *Additional Resources* that will help you go deeper in learning about that specific topic.

HOW TO THINK FROM HEAVEN'S PERSPECTIVE

*"Jesus urged us to do an about-face in our approach to
reality because His Kingdom is at hand. He brought His
world with Him, and it's within our reach. He wants
you to see reality from God's perspective, to learn to live
from His world toward the visible world. But if you
don't change the way you think, you'll never be able to
apprehend the Kingdom power that is available."*

VIDEO LISTENING GUIDE

1. Your beginning with Christ started with ___repentance___.

2. Repentance: A godly sorrow over sin that produces a _shift_ in how we think and see reality.

3. You know your mind is renewed when the _impossible_ looks logical.

4. Faith does not come from the mind; it comes from the ___heart___.

5. The renewed mind _enchances_ faith.

6. Jesus' transfiguration is a ___representation___ of what the renewed mind looks like.

7. Thoughts ___enpower___ the invisible—the unseen world.

8. There is a difference between what is in our ___possesion___ and what is in our account.

Keys to Thinking from Heaven's Perspective

1. The renewed mind starts with how we think about ___God/Him___.

2. The renewed mind recognizes that God has ___answers___ to every problem and He has made these solutions available to us.

EMBRACE YOUR NEW NORMAL

But if the Spirit of Him who raised Jesus from the dead dwells in you, He who raised Christ from the dead will also give life to your mortal bodies through His Spirit who dwells in you (ROMANS 8:11).

The journey of the renewed mind begins with a reorientation of our thoughts toward the fundamental expression of Christianity. If Romans 8:11 is indeed true, and the Spirit of the resurrected Christ actually does live inside of me, I must conclude that powerless Christianity is inexcusable and unacceptable. It is also unnecessary. In the days ahead, the goal is simple. We are going to discover what it means to think from God's perspective and how to embrace this as our *new normal* demonstration of the Christian life.

Momentum is increasing across the earth. As believers embrace the invitation of the renewed mind, what used to be abnormal or uncommon is increasing in frequency. Miracles are happening all over the world on a weekly, if not daily basis. The level of breakthrough we used to yearn for, we are now seeing happen with consistency. It is a revolutionary approach to Christian living—a return to the authentic.

What is causing this shift? It is not something new. If anything, believers are embracing the foundational perspective that the disciples of Christ maintained as they turned the world upside down after Pentecost. Romans 8:11 was not some theology, concept, or idea to them. Rather, these men and women who walked with Jesus and watched what He did recognized that they received the *same* Holy Spirit who empowered Jesus to perform the miracles, signs, and wonders that He walked in.

The same lifestyle is available to you *today*.

TRANSFORMATION THOUGHT

God is inviting you to embrace a new normal. Your experience and expression of Christianity was always designed to be supernatural!

REFLECTION QUESTIONS

1. What do you think it means to "reorient your thinking" to embrace the expression of Christianity that Romans 8:11 talks about?

    a. _____

    _____

    b. _____

    _____

    c. _____

    _____

    d. _____

    _____

    e. _____

    _____

2. Why do you think people experience an increased measure of the supernatural when they change the way they think about what it means to have the Spirit of God living inside of them?

    a. _____

    _____

    b. _____

    _____

    c. _____

    _____

    d. _____

    _____

TRANSFORMATION PRAYER

Thank You, Father, that the same Holy Spirit who raised Jesus from the dead also lives inside of me—and empowers me to live the life that Jesus modeled!

ADDITIONAL RESOURCES

The Ascended Life
http://store.ibethel.org/p7869/the-ascended-life

" Learn to identify the originals "Van Gogh" = Bible
" I never analyse my faith I act upon it."
" He doesn't wring his hands over stuff."
" God has answers + He has them for me."

Romans 12,1:
Luke 9:29 transfiguration = Renewed mind.
2 Corinth. 10:5

DISCOVER GOD'S WILL

And as you go, preach, saying, "The kingdom of heaven is at hand." Heal the sick, cleanse the lepers, raise the dead, cast out demons. Freely you have received, freely give (MATTHEW 10:7-8).

One of the most frequent questions that we entertain in our minds is, "What is God's will for my life?" How we begin to answer this question shapes everything in regard to how we walk out our everyday Christian lives. The good news is that we don't need to go through our entire lives waiting for divine direction that may or may not come down from Heaven, giving us a play-by-play of God's will for our entire lives. Jesus revealed it through His lifestyle and we have it recorded in the Gospels.

In Matthew 10:7-8, Jesus gives you and me a clear picture of God's will for our lives. However, to embrace the invitation that He is extending, we need to change the way we think about God's will. Often, we are waiting for the Holy Spirit to tell us something like, "Work at *this* job," or, "Go off to *this* country." We are waiting for specifics—and yes, there are times where He will clearly reveal such information—when in fact, the essentials are revealed right there in the example of Jesus Christ.

What is God's will? Wherever we go and whatever we do, our foremost commitment is to the mandate of Jesus, which is to preach and demonstrate the Kingdom. *Heal the sick, cleanse the lepers, raise the dead, cast out demons.* This is normal Christianity in action. What has happened in the past is that we have reduced our definition of normal to agree with what we have been experiencing. The problem with this perspective is that we will go on experiencing an old level of normal *until* we redefine our expectation of normal, and place a demand on our experience to come in alignment with the lifestyle defined by Jesus.

This is what we are moving toward. God's will actually begins with us changing the way we think about God's will, and elevating our perspective to embrace what Jesus commissioned us to do as foundational expressions of God's will. Everything else will flow from that core revelation.

TRANSFORMATION THOUGHT

Jesus taught and showed us what God's will is for our lives—preach and demonstrate the Kingdom of God.

REFLECTION QUESTIONS

1. How does this perspective change the way you approach the question, "What is God's will for my life?"

_____

_____

_____

_____

2. What type of freedom does this bring to you?

Peace in knowing it's all good. Steadfast in the Lord, Look beyond all circumstances, be depth of whose are in Christ. Hope to live in freedom. Contentment, Joy.

TRANSFORMATION PRAYER

Holy Spirit, thank You for making it possible for me to know and do the will of God. Wherever I go and whatever I do, help me to preach and demonstrate the Kingdom!

ADDITIONAL RESOURCES

When Heaven Invades Earth
http://store.ibethel.org/p6685/when-heaven-invades-earth

HOW TO PROVE GOD'S WILL

Be transformed by the renewing of your mind, that
you may prove what is that good and acceptable
and perfect will of God (ROMANS 12:2).

One of the major functions of miracles and supernatural living is to offer immediate, irrefutable proof of what God wants to happen on earth. It demonstrates who God is by idsplaying what His reality looks like.

Yesterday, we looked at some different ways you and I can walk in God's will for our lives. Ultimately, it all goes back to His primary agenda, which is made clear in Matthew 6:10—*on earth as it is in heaven*. Our mission is to show earth what Heaven looks like, and Heaven is a climate and culture defined by the Presence of the King. Everything in Heaven functions the way it does because it is all marked by the Presence of the One seated upon the Throne of Heaven.

When Heaven comes to earth, bringing with it the miraculous demonstration of the Kingdom, we are actually participating in proving God's will—showing the world what He looks like. While we need to tell the world who the King is, we are also responsible for revealing Him through demonstration. The lifestyle Jesus modeled consisted of both preaching and power, with one not overruling the other.

Most people don't know how God behaves, or what's inside His heart for each one of us. Your calling and my calling as believers may be too massive to fully understand, but the Bible's command is clear: Our job is to demonstrate that the reality which exists in Heaven can be manifested right here, right now. We are not just to be people who believe correct things about God, but people who put the will of God on display, expressing it and causing others to realize, "Oh, so that's what God is like." Healing and deliverance and restoration do much more than solve the immediate problem; they give people a concrete demonstration of who God is.

TRANSFORMATION THOUGHT

When you supernaturally demonstrate God's Kingdom, you show the world what the King looks like—you put God's nature on display!

REFLECTION QUESTIONS

1. How do you understand this idea of proving God's will?

_____

_____

_____

2. Why do you think that demonstrating the Kingdom—through healing, deliverance, miracles, etc.—is such an effective way of showing the world what God is like?

Show Love, It authenticates God (The Kingdom) "Worlds way is seeing is believing or I don't believe what I don't see!

TRANSFORMATION PRAYER

Father, I know the commission to represent You is great—but You have empowered me greatly with the Holy Spirit! Help me to prove Your will and show the world who You are by demonstrating Your power.

ADDITIONAL RESOURCES

Supernatural Courage

http://store.ibethel.org/p3643/supernatural-courage

Day Four

THINKING WELL IS IMPORTANT

...be transformed by the renewing of
your mind... (ROMANS 12:2).

Our minds must be transformed to demonstrate a Kingdom lifestyle. The process begins when we recognize the value of investing in the mind. As people, we invest in what we value.

This is why it is important that as believers, we actually emphasize the mind appropriately, rather than reject it. Sometimes, there is a tendency in a supernatural culture to downplay the mind and focus mainly on experience. The mind becomes devalued in exchange for upholding faith, as some teach that the mind can be a stumbling block to walking in the miraculous. The result? The mind ends up taking a back seat to the supernatural.

The problem is that the mind and how we think are actually vital keys to walking in a sustained supernatural lifestyle. Rejecting them is costly. Isolated miracles are definitely worthy of celebration, but our inheritance is a life that is followed by a continuous flow of supernatural demonstration. This is the authentic expression of Christianity we are looking to bring to the world.

I understand that there is often hesitancy when we talk about the mind as a tool of God. At times in church history the intellectual aspect of the mind has been so exalted that it has wiped out a real lifestyle of faith. The mind itself is not our enemy; it is the un-renewed thought patterns that need to be transformed and shaped to align with God's thinking. When operating in agreement with the perspective of Heaven, the mind is an incredibly powerful asset.

Remember, the only way to consistently do Kingdom works is to view reality from God's perspective. That's what the Bible means when it talks about renewing our minds. The battle is in the mind. The mind is the essential tool in bringing Kingdom reality to the problems and crisis people face. God has made your mind to be the gatekeeper of the supernatural!

TRANSFORMATION THOUGHT

The mind is a valuable asset to believers, enabling them to think from Heaven's perspective and live a supernatural lifestyle.

REFLECTION QUESTIONS

1. Why is it so important that, as believers, we start to value the mind again? What happens when we don't?

_____

_____

_____

_____

2. How do you think renewing our minds and thinking from Heaven's perspective enables us to live out a sustained supernatural lifestyle, versus a Christian life that may experience occasional miracles, here and there?

By thing that doesn't have fuel dies.
God's fuel is a never ending tank
we go from Glory to glory. Perspuctive comes
thru prayer!

our mind (what we believe) dictates
how we think in the natural.
our thought life is based on our
experiences

TRANSFORMATION PRAYER

Holy Spirit, show me the value of investing in my mind and thinking in agreement with the Father. I want to see everything from Your perspective.

ADDITIONAL RESOURCES

The Supernatural Power of a Renewed Mind
http://store.ibethel.org/p59/the-supernatural-power-of-a-renewed-mind

"Thinking from the Throne" 10:30 A.M., June 09, 2013
http://store.ibethel.org/p7622/thinking-from-the
-throne-10-30am-june-09-2013

THE ENTRYWAY OF REPENTANCE

From that time Jesus began to preach and to say, "Repent,
for the kingdom of heaven is at hand" (MATTHEW 4:17).

Having a renewed mind is often not an issue of whether or not someone is going to Heaven, but of how much of Heaven one wants to experience in his or her life right now. When Jesus began His public ministry, He announced that the coming of the Kingdom would require repentance. In order to access and walk in the Kingdom lifestyle Jesus modeled and made available, it is important for us to have a proper perspective on repentance.

It is true that repentance begins in a place of godly sorrow over sin. The message of the Gospel pierces the deepest parts of our being and we are, in the most wonderful way possible, overwhelmed by the extravagant goodness of God. He does not come with condemnation. Scripture reminds us that it is the *"goodness of God leads you to repentance"* (Rom. 2:4). In light of the pure, extreme, relentless goodness of God, we recognize that sin, and a lifestyle of sin, pale in comparison to the glory of knowing the One who rescued and redeemed us.

This expression of repentance gains us entry into the Kingdom, which is absolutely vital. However, I am convinced that most Christians have repented enough to be forgiven, but not enough to *see* the Kingdom. This does not imply there is some other "work" that needs to be done. It is simply possessing a complete understanding of the wonderful reality of repentance. Not only does it introduce us to an entire new world called the Kingdom of God, but actually shows us how to live in this realm as *our* new reality. When Jesus preached a message of "repentance," He was inviting people to experience the Greek concept of *metanoeō,* which means to "change one's mind."

Meeting Jesus at conversion was the first step in your Christian walk. Now, it's time to watch what took place in your spirit transform every part of your life—this includes changing your mind! Biblical repentance changes the way we think in order to agree with how God thinks. Our lives begin to follow these new Kingdom thought patterns and we begin to live the miraculous life that Jesus made available.

TRANSFORMATION THOUGHT

Repentance is not just feeling godly sorrow over sin; it is the transformation of our minds to think like God does in order to see and experience His Kingdom on earth.

REFLECTION QUESTIONS

1. What does the following statement mean to you: "Most Christians have repented enough to be forgiven, but not enough to see the Kingdom"? What does it look like to be forgiven of sin, but still not experience the power of the Kingdom of God?

     a. You can be forgiven but have you repented.

     b. Lack of intimacy.
     True repentance allows the

     c. shift + transformation.

     d. _____

2. How does this understanding of repentance change the way you personally approach repentance in your life?

a. _____

_____

b. _____

_____

c. _____

_____

d. _____

_____

TRANSFORMATION PRAYER

Holy Spirit, thank You for changing the way I think. Show me how to a live a lifestyle of repentance, where my mind is constantly being transformed to agree with, and reflect, God's thoughts. Fill my mind with Your thoughts so I can experience and live out Your Kingdom realities on earth.

ADDITIONAL RESOURCES

"Mt. Transfiguration: Kingdom Come" 11:00 A.M., October 21, 2012
http://store.ibethel.org/p6714/mt-transfiguration-kingdom-come
-11-00am-october-21-2012

YOUR MIND, GOD'S DWELLING PLACE

"I am incredibly excited about the revolution I see taking place in the Church. We are again becoming the dwelling place of God that was promised in the Bible. We have hungered for more, prayed for more, and now we are receiving unprecedented insight into our privileges and responsibilities in the Kingdom of God. These insights aren't just being pondered; people are acting on them, and more and more, God's will is being done on earth as it is in Heaven."

"Faith is to explore
what revelation reveals."

Todi:

Having a transformed
mind means we also
have a transformed
imagination + be
subjects to His
incredible imagination"

Be creative!!
God has no
barriers.

VIDEO LISTENING GUIDE   *201*

1. The more we discover how God thinks, the more it opens us up to
   experience . Him differently.

2. We _restrict_ what God is capable of doing in a situation because of our thought life.

3. The way we think either _cooperates_ with God, or resists Him.

4. If we entertain thoughts in our minds that God does not entertain, we are entertaining a _lie_ .

5. When we believe a lie, we _empower_ the liar.

6. The house of God is built on the edge of two _worlds_ .

7. Jesus was the initial _Fullfillment_ . of the prophetic picture in Genesis 28.

8. The renewed mind enables us to live from God's _World_ toward our world.

9. Whenever we speak God's words, we change people's _options_ .

10. God can act independently of us, but He has chosen to _partner_ with us.

11. Faith is to _explore_ what revelation reveals.

Gate transition place between 2 worlds   *House of God - Gate transition gate from one word to another*

13 - Gen 28:16.

Gen. 28 - Jacobs Ladder
Rom. 8   1st mention of God's house - no mention of a building   physical

A renewed mind is not peripheral -   building
prophesy of the new testament + what world

John 6 - Jesus Spirit made Flesh.
my words are Spirit
manifest The
John 1 - 30-51   H.S. Hself
Tabernacle -
Acts 2:2-3
(Angels) · Heb 1-7
Gate of 2 worlds.   Psalm 104,4.
Citizenship in 2 worlds   Wind/Fire.

- Angelic Activity
- Co-laboring partnership ā God to release
      His purposes thru that gate.

★ Kingdom of God is _in_ the H.S.

"_Presence_ goes out + captures hearts"
"Quest to learn what God is saying is _vital_."
"Words are always releasing power/
                                    presence"
"As soon as you speak truth to them they
   are presently presence
   you chase the opress of how
   that person lives + you did it
   simply by decree"

RETHINKING GOD'S HOUSE

Then Jacob awoke from his sleep and said, "Surely the Lord is in this place, and I did not know it." And he was afraid and said, "How awesome is this place! This is none other than the house of God, and this is the gate of heaven!" (GENESIS 28:16-17)

To effectively walk out the Kingdom lifestyle that Jesus modeled and made possible for us, one of the first things we need to re-evaluate is what we think about the *house of God*. Our concept of God's house is absolutely vital to whether or not we take up the charge to bring Heaven to earth, drawing from the unlimited resources of God's Kingdom supply.

In Genesis 28, during Jacob's dream, we see the first mention of the concept *house of God* in Scripture. Interestingly enough, there is no building. There is no organization. There is simply a man and God. Jacob was there, God was there, and according to Genesis 28:12, there was *"a ladder…set up on the earth, and its top reached to heaven; and there the angels of God were ascending and descending on it."* There was a constant flow of supernatural resources being delivered from one world to the next. For a more extensive study on the nature of what was taking place in this context, see the *Hosting the Presence* curriculum and book.

For now, we need to focus on how our minds embrace this idea, *the house of God*. What does it look like to you? The church actually houses the *house of God*. A building is not the house of God, but rather, the people who visit that building for services and different activities are the house of God. Because of Jesus, man has become God's dwelling place on the earth. This perspective changes everything. Instead of doing everything possible to just get people to come into a building to experience God, we have the ability to bring the encounter right to them.

When the *house of God* becomes mobile, we then change the way we think of the expression of church entirely. While we celebrate the fruitfulness of our corporate gatherings and the community that is built in that context, most of the supernatural ministry that our church participates in takes place outside of the four walls of the building structure. Why? Because, like the countless others across the earth who are awakening to their identity, we are embracing God's blueprint for what His house was designed to look like—people who carry God's presence into the earth and transform the world around them.

TRANSFORMATION THOUGHT

The house of God is not a structure, building, or organization— God's dwelling place on earth is inside of redeemed humanity.

REFLECTION QUESTIONS

1. How have you thought about the house of God in the past?

_____

_____

_____

_____

2. What happens when you start believing—and living like—you are the dwelling place of God on the earth? How does this change the way you see ministry?

_____ we see kingdom life, see restoration. _____

_____

_____

_____

TRANSFORMATION PRAYER

Father, thank You for making it possible for me to be Your dwelling place on earth. Thank You for sending the Holy Spirit to come live inside of me and make me Your house. Show me how to live this out and bring an encounter with You to the world.

ADDITIONAL RESOURCES

Revival Outside the Camp

http://store.ibethel.org/p266/revival-outside-the-camp

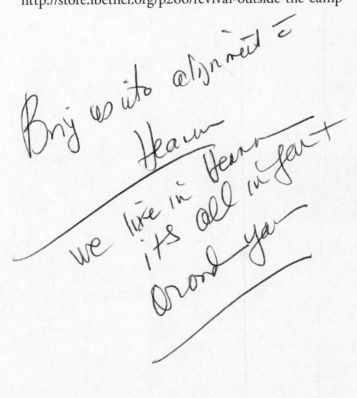

RETHINKING OPEN HEAVENS

In those days Jesus came from Nazareth of Galilee and was baptized by John in the Jordan. And when he came up out of the water, immediately he saw the heavens being torn open and the Spirit descending on him like a dove (MARK 1:9-10 ESV).

How many of us have prayed, *"Lord, rend the heavens and come down"*? This passage comes out of Isaiah 64:1, and so powerfully reflects our hearts' great longing—to see His presence released with greater measures of power and transformative results in the world. While the motive for praying this way is pure, Isaiah 64:1 is actually a prayer that has already been fulfilled. Today, I want to invite you to change the way you think about open heavens and what they mean to you.

This is a subject that we are intentional about. So much has been made available to us because of Jesus. In Mark 1:9-10, we see that Isaiah 64:1 was answered at Jesus' baptism. To *rend the heavens* is actually a violent act. Heaven is torn open, and that which has been contained behind the veil is released into the earth. This is exactly what happened at Jesus' baptism, for finally a Man appeared on the scene who could be the first fit dwelling place for the Holy Spirit. History had been waiting and longing for this very moment.

Recall that in the Old Testament, the Holy Spirit came upon people for a season, time, or task, but He did not remain. He could not. There was no abiding Presence of God upon humanity because of the barrier of sin. However, when Jesus came onto the scene, perfection entered the equation—perfection that was completely accommodating to the abiding Presence of like-perfection. Jesus, the sinless and holy Man, was fit to host the *Holy* Spirit of God. Surely, this is why Heaven was torn open that day. It long awaited the era when God's true dwelling place would be established.

Heaven has not closed since that day. Jesus lived and ministered under an open heaven, and now, because the same Spirit that lived in Jesus lives inside of us, we walk under that same open heaven. It's no longer necessary for us to cry out for an open heaven, for it's already a reality for every single believer who has the Holy Spirit living within them. Are there greater expressions and demonstrations of this reality we long to see? Yes. In the meantime, we celebrate what we have already received because of Jesus. Instead of crying out for what we already have, we rise up and steward the wonderful blessing that the Holy Spirit has made accessible to all followers of Christ—a life *under* an open heaven.

TRANSFORMATION THOUGHT

Jesus fulfilled the cry of Isaiah 64:1 on the day of His baptism. Heaven was torn open, and has not closed since. Instead of asking for an open heaven, we now live under what Jesus made available and what the Holy Spirit makes accessible to all believers.

REFLECTION QUESTIONS

1. What does an "open heaven" look like to you? What did it look like for Jesus and how do you think it impacted His life and ministry?

_____

_____

_____

_____

2. Why is it important to understand that we already have an open heaven, and don't need to keep on asking for this reality over our lives?

_____

_____

_____

_____

TRANSFORMATION PRAYER

Holy Spirit, thank You for empowering me to live under an open heaven where the power and resources of Heaven flow into the earth! Show me how to steward this reality in an even greater measure.

ADDITIONAL RESOURCES

Mission Possible
http://store.ibethel.org/p308/mission-possible

RETHINKING THE BELIEVER'S MANDATE

This is none other than the house of God, and
this is the gate of heaven! (GENESIS 28:17)

In Genesis 28:17, Jacob uses language that finds fulfillment in a corresponding New Testament reality. Today, I want us to look at this concept, *the gate of heaven*. This is not some new way to salvation; Jesus was, is, and forever will be the only gateway to Heaven. He is the Way, the Truth, and the Life. This is not about getting to Jesus, but more so about getting Jesus to the world. Once we receive Christ, we actually became the gate of heaven on the earth. This all starts in our minds—specifically, what we think about the gravity of what we received at salvation and who we became as God's dwelling place.

In this context and elsewhere in the Bible, "gate" seems to mark a place of transition and access. In the natural you might walk through a gate to go from your front yard to the sidewalk, or from your backyard to your driveway. In the same way, when we talk about the Church being the gate of heaven, we are referring to the place where the reality of His dominion becomes available for all of mankind—His world invades ours!

Now here is where our thinking demands a significant adjustment. In Matthew 16:18-19, Jesus introduces the reality of the "gates of hell." For so many of us, we have this picture of the Church as a group of people locked inside a compound, shoulders against the gate, trying to hold the fort as the devil and his powerful minions beat against it. We see the Church in a posture of fear and weakness, trying to protect what we have until God comes and rescues us from the big, bad devil. This perspective is the breeding ground for escapist theology, where we are just holding on until Jesus comes back to take us away from a planet on a path to destruction. This is the exact opposite of how we need to embrace our identity as the house of God, *the gate of heaven*. If anything, we are God's ambassadors of restoration, wholeness and healing. The very people who actually carry the solutions to the problems that confront this planet cannot afford to hide away, waiting for it all to end.

We also cannot afford to stop short of Jesus' powerful assurance, *"and the gates of hell shall not prevail against it* (the church)." We are not living on the defensive, but the offense. As the gate of heaven, we are not simply holding up these huge iron doors, shielding and protecting us from every assault of the devil; we are opening the gates and releasing the increase of Heaven's transformative dominion on earth.

TRANSFORMATION THOUGHT

As the body of Christ, we are the gate of heaven on the earth—carrying divine solutions to the problems that humanity is facing.

REFLECTION QUESTIONS

1. What does this reality look like to you—the church as the "gate of heaven"?

_____

_____

_____

_____

2. Why is it important for us to think about the church in the correct way when it comes to being the "gate of Heaven" and responding to the "gates of hell"?

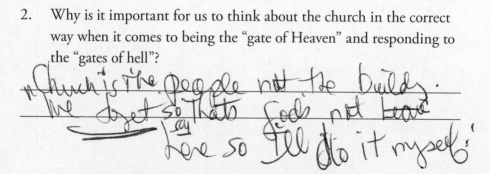

TRANSFORMATION PRAYER

Father, I step into my identity as the gate of Your world on the earth. I am a point of access. I do not live my life on the defense against the enemy, but because of the Holy Spirit living in me, I release the love, presence, and power of Jesus into every situation and circumstance I come across. Increase Your reign and rule through my life.

ADDITIONAL RESOURCES

Releasing the Kingdom
http://store.ibethel.org/p253/releasing-the-kingdom

"The Gate of Heaven" 6:00 P.M., December 23, 2012
http://store.ibethel.org/p7055/the-gate-of-heaven-6-00pm
-december-23-2012

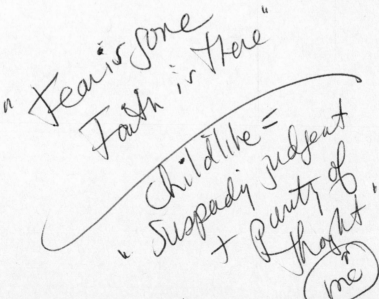

RETHINKING BINDING AND LOOSING

I will give you the keys of the kingdom of heaven; and whatever you bind on earth shall have been bound in heaven, and whatever you loose on earth shall have been loosed in heaven (MATTHEW 16:19 NASB).

This is one of the more accurate translations of this verse. Due to some confusion, some have gotten carried away with the idea of binding and loosing, believing that whatever they "loose" through prayer or declaration—regardless of whether it's in agreement with God's heart or not—will come to pass just because they are "loosing" it on earth, and as a result, it gets loosed in Heaven. We don't tell God what to do. There is an order that we are bringing ourselves into agreement and alignment with. This is what produces supernatural confidence in us—the fact that we are binding and loosing in agreement with God's will and purpose. The key is rethinking this concept of binding and loosing by understanding Heaven's blueprint.

We loose on earth that which has been loosed in Heaven already. Likewise, we bind, or forbid that which has already been bound in Heaven. The model is *on earth as it is in Heaven*. The question is: What is loosed in Heaven? What permeates the culture and climate of God's world? Peace. Wholeness. Joy. Conversely, what is forbidden in Heaven? Sickness. Torment. Oppression. We are not telling God what to bind or loose in Heaven. Rather, we are commanding situations on earth to come into divine alignment with the realities that are established by the Father in Heaven. Again, we are not commanding God. If anything, what's present and absent in Heaven is God's command to what should be present or absent on earth. Again, if *on earth as it is in Heaven* is His model and standard, this is the reality we need to be pressing into. We do this through binding and loosing.

I want you to rethink this even further. More than commanding, it's really the process of agreement. What we bind on earth or loose on earth is based on our agreement with God's world, and God's blueprint. Heaven is our standard. Our citizenship is first in God's Kingdom, and as His ambassadors, we are called to expand the reach of His Kingdom to the uttermost parts of the earth. We disciple nations on how to experience the rule and reign of Heaven in every sphere of society, not through military takeover or violent overthrow, but by introducing this world to the realities that are normal in Heaven—peace, joy, wholeness, rest, abundance, creativity, etc.

TRANSFORMATION THOUGHT

Our assignment is to bind what has already been bound in Heaven, and loose what is already loosed in Heaven.

REFLECTION QUESTIONS

1. What does "binding and loosing" look like to you?

   a. _____

   _____

   b. _____

   _____

   c. _____

   _____

2. Why do you think that it is important to first discover what is bound/loosed in Heaven before binding/loosing on earth? How do you know what's already bound/loosed in Heaven?

   _____

   _____

TRANSFORMATION PRAYER

Thank You for the ability to see what is loosed and what is bound in Heaven, so that I can bring these realities to earth. Increase revelation and clarity when it comes to studying Your Word, and discovering what life looks like in Heaven, so that I can release this same quality of life on earth.

ADDITIONAL RESOURCES

Heaven: Our Model for Life and Ministry Here on Earth
http://store.ibethel.org/p40/heaven-our-model-for-life
-and-ministry-here-on-earth

RETHINKING THE TEMPLE OF GOD

For you are the temple of the living God. As God has said:
"I will dwell in them and walk among them. I will be their
God, and they shall be My people" (2 CORINTHIANS 6:16).

We conclude this week adding to what we started out discovering—the house of God is not a structure composed of bricks and mortar, but it is redeemed humanity being filled with the Presence of the Holy Spirit. The first reality we needed to rethink was what the house of God *looked like*. Now, I want us to rethink what the temple of God operates like in the twenty-first century.

In Second Corinthians 6, Paul is actually quoting God. Such a statement demands special attention! God's desire was to dwell inside of His people and walk among them. This concept of *walk among* is intriguing. In the Old Testament, the temple was in a fixed position. It did not get up and change geographies. Now, because of the redemptive work of Christ and the infilling of the Holy Spirit, the temple of God has become mobile. We now carry the glory that remained stationary in the temple. This is what we need to rethink if we are going to bring God to those who are not necessarily looking for Him.

It is amazing to think that we carry the Presence that filled the temple. There are countless people whom we encounter, day after day, who will never come to church. Some may. But many will not, and to these people, we have the distinct honor of bringing the temple of God directly to their lives through our contact. to them.

We see this pictured in the Old Testament—God's Presence cannot be moved by some structure, organization, or system created by man.

Consider that the church building is stationary. It is a place of fellowship, equipping, teaching, and yes, transformation, but when all is said and done, the physical building cannot uproot itself and go to where the people in need are. This is our unique privilege, for we carry what no building ever could—God's Presence.

Back in Second Samuel 6, we see what happened when man assumed that his systems or structures were adequate to transport God's glorious Presence. The people experienced disastrous results (see 2 Sam. 6:6-8). This is because no structure humanity can create, regardless of how beautiful or ingenious, can truly carry God's Presence. Even in the Old Testament, the appropriate protocol involved priests carrying the Ark of the Covenant upon their shoulders. In the New Testament, because of Jesus' blood, we are all priests. We have been cleansed of sin and became fit to carry God's Presence to those who need to encounter Him.

TRANSFORMATION THOUGHT

The temple of God is no longer a fixed structure; the Holy Spirit made it possible for all believers to carry the Presence of God wherever they go.

REFLECTION QUESTIONS

1. What happens when we change the way we see God's temple—from a fixed structure to people filled with the Holy Spirit? How does this change the way we relate to the world and those who need ministry?

_____

_____

_____

_____

2. As God's portable temple, what are you able to offer the world?

_____

_____

TRANSFORMATION PRAYER

Father, thank You for making me Your temple. No longer does Your presence rest in a building or structure; You have made Your people Your resting place. It is a great honor to carry Your Presence and bring people into an encounter with Your love and Your Kingdom.

ADDITIONAL RESOURCES

Hosting the Presence
http://store.ibethel.org/p6558/hosting-the-presence

KEYS TO GROWING IN REVELATION

"This is the nature of revelation—it opens up new realms of living, of possibility, of faith. It is absolutely impossible to live the normal Christian life without receiving regular revelation from God."

"The willingness to obey the rule
is what attracts the
revelation."

"God is inviting me into the process."

— altogether —
"There is a constant motion...
it never stops"

(H.S. → us
us H.S. God
us H.S. God)

Math 16, 13-17

"Receiving
revelation" Math 11:25
Luke 10:21

Psalm 131:1

"Self criticism"
a counterfeit of humility

1 Corth 2:9

God hides things for
us + above us
see it is
glorifying God.
1 Corth
2:9

The greatest search engine in the universe is the Holy Spirit. Look for this in the heart of the Father + when he finds them he brings them to you.

Week Three

VIDEO LISTENING GUIDE

Roadblocks to Revelation

1. Humanity without Christ in the center is __demonic__ in nature.

Unhealthy

2. __Ambition__ can take you into the mind of man without you even knowing it.

What Is True Meditation?

1. Biblical meditation is to __ponder__ something over and over again. *"Cow chewing it's cud."*

2. Biblical meditation is the __atmosphere__ in which revelation thrives.

Keys to Accessing Revelation

1. Childlikeness __attracts__ revelation.
   - Every move of God starts with the __poor__ in spirit.
   - The drive to be __profound__ ruins one's ability to hear from God.

2. The willingness to __obey__ attracts revelation.

3. We must be on the same __frequency__ as God in order to hear what He is saying.

Cultivate a childlike spirit.

Your royalty is demonstrated when we have legal access to the mysteries of God.

His thoughts — out number the sand on the seashore.

Surrender + Obedience or Obidence (private)

1 Cor 2:9-12

REVELATION: THINKING FROM HEAVEN TO EARTH

*Where there is no revelation, the people
cast off restraint* (PROVERBS 29:18).

This week, I want us to explore the value and absolute necessity of revelation in our lives as believers. It is revelation that brings relevance to what we already know and it is the process of revelation that brings our thinking into agreement with Heaven. Revelation is not some new addition to Scripture. Rather, it is the Holy Spirit giving us specific insight and instruction on how to apply Scripture to our everyday lives. He brings greater clarity when it comes to the eternal, unchanging Word of the Lord, for only the Spirit of God can grant you and me access to the understanding of God (see 1 Cor. 2:10-12).

A more correct and complete translation of the Proverbs 29:18 passage would read something like this, "Without a prophetic revelation, the people go unrestrained, walking in circles, having no certain destiny."

Revelation gives you and me the ability to see *right now* from God's vantage point. This is how it gives the Word of God present relevance. This is not a nice vitamin pill we can take or leave. This is what we live by. Revelation is so essential in our lives that without it we perish. Without unfolding prophetic revelation that expands your capacity to see life from God's perspective, you will perish. Without seeing your present circumstances through God's eyes, you will spiritually die.

Revelation is the process of starting to think from God's perspective and vantage point. It is so much more than memorizing

Scripture. As mentioned at the beginning of this study, it is experiencing a complete reorientation of the way we think. We are no longer thinking from earth to earth, trying to explain what we are currently dealing with from a natural perspective, but instead, we are thinking from Heaven to earth. We see everything in the now from the eternal perspective of Heaven.

Thinking from earth to earth endeavors to bring solutions from the un-renewed mind. When we start thinking from Heaven toward earth, we tap into the flow of revelation. We start seeing things differently. This is where impossibilities are transformed into opportunities for miracles. However, we will go on seeing the impossible as impossible when we consider it from a natural, earthly perspective. Revelation is the process through which our thinking is actually called up higher and brought into alignment with the thoughts of God.

TRANSFORMATION THOUGHT

Revelation is thinking from Heaven to earth, seeing everything we experience on earth from the perspective and vantage point of Heaven.

REFLECTION QUESTIONS

1. How do you understand the process of thinking from Heaven to earth? Can you give an example of what you think this process looks like?

_____

_____

_____

_____

2. How does revelation give us greater understanding and clarity on the Bible?

_____

_____

_____

_____

TRANSFORMATION PRAYER

Lord, I ask that You would give to me the spirit of wisdom and revelation in the knowledge of You. Transform my mind to think from Heaven to earth, so that I see everything in this life from the lens of Your perspective.

ADDITIONAL RESOURCES

Faith Anchored in the Unseen
http://store.ibethel.org/p1594/faith-anchored-in-the-unseen

REVELATION TUNES YOU IN TO GOD'S FREQUENCY

Now we have received, not the spirit of the world, but the
Spirit who is from God, that we might know the things that
have been freely given to us by God (1 CORINTHIANS 2:12).

The invitation to you and I remains the same as it was to the apostle John on the island of Patmos, *"Come up here"* (Rev. 4:1). I want us to explore what it looks like and how it works to think from Heaven to earth. First, it demands an elevated perspective. We must proactively choose to see life from God's point of view. In order to do this, we need to tune in to His frequency.

Think of it this way. Right now in the room where you're sitting, movies are playing all around you. If you had the right receiver or satellite dish, you could pick them up. Just because you can't see the waves passing through doesn't mean they aren't there. With the right receiver you could watch any number of television shows, ball games, talk shows, or listen to private conversations on cell phones and short wave radio. But without the proper receiver, you won't pick up anything. The key is activating the proper receiver so you can *tune in* to what's going on in the atmosphere around you.

Scripture tells us that the natural man does not receive the things of the Spirit of God (see 1 Cor. 2:14). Using a radio analogy, if God is speaking on FM radio and we are on AM, we can turn that dial all the way to the left, then go slowly over every station. We can quote verses with every turn of the dial. We can claim the promises of God. We can do anything we want to, but as long as we are on AM and He is on FM, we are not going to receive His message because the natural man is still receiving. The key to unlocking revelation on God's frequency is to become spiritually discerning—to open our spirit man to receive direct revelation from God.

To a large degree, we need to stop fighting to receive revelation and simply yield to the Holy Spirit. In our own human ability, we cannot pick up on divine revelation. It's impossible. However, it is the Spirit of God who searches the deep things of God and then makes them known to us. We will constantly frustrate ourselves and come up short if we think we are able to access the deep things of God, even by using some of the strategies I mentioned earlier. Those things are useful, but they will never help us cross the AM to FM gulf; it is only the Holy Spirit who can bring us there. I invite you to surrender to Him today. Ask Him to come and bring you into the depths of revelation that only He can make available. It is His delight to do it.

TRANSFORMATION THOUGHT

No human works or striving can grant us access to the revelation and deep things of God—only the Holy Spirit can communicate these things to us, and this takes place by yielding to Him.

REFLECTION QUESTIONS

1. How does yielding to the Holy Spirit get rid of frustration when it comes to receiving revelation from God?

_____

_____

_____

_____

2. What does the process of receiving revelation look like to you? What are a few ways the Holy Spirit reveals things to you, in your everyday life?

_____

_____

_____

_____

TRANSFORMATION PRAYER

Holy Spirit, You are the One who searches and knows the deep things of God. Thank You that You have made these realities available to me! I cannot search them out for myself; it is You who brings the revelation to me.

ADDITIONAL RESOURCES

Recognizing His Voice
http://store.ibethel.org/p2990/recognizing-his-voice

Day Thirteen

KEYS TO RECOGNIZING AND RECEIVING REVELATION

...knowledge is easy to one who has
understanding (Proverbs 14:6 NASB).

In order to recognize when we are receiving revelation, we need to maintain an understanding of how God speaks. Here are a few ways you can recognize revelation in your everyday life.

One, when you receive revelation, it will have a freshness to it. It's the classic example of someone reading a passage in Scripture they have read a "million times," or hearing a pastor share about a topic they have heard repeated frequently, but for some special reason, there is a freshness about what they are reading or hearing. These are just two examples, but in both cases, there is a freshness and timeliness to the words being read or heard.

Two, revelation always sounds better than anything we could have come up with in our own ability or intellect. Has that ever happened when you were saying something, and as you were speaking, your mind was actually impressed with what was coming out of your mouth—as if the words were not your own? In those moments, you are operating in the flow of revelation.

Three, revelation releases supernatural invasions of peace into the midst of calamity, confusion, or torment. Someone speaks to you and it is exactly what you needed for just that moment. It was as if the person was sharing something that was tailored specifically to you and your situation. This is revelation in action.

Next, I want to give you two practical ways you can position yourself to receive revelation.

First, build a solid support structure upon the Word of God. Scripture gives us foundational pillars to build our lives on. As we build on what has already been revealed, we position ourselves to receive what is *yet* to be revealed. Remember, God is not *adding* to Scripture, but bringing timely clarity and prophetic relevance to His Word for your specific situation, decision, or circumstance.

Second, respond to the known through obedience. The desire for an increase in revelation should always be coupled with an attitude of stewardship for what you have already received and obedience to what God has already said. Your obedience tells God, "I'm ready to go to the next step." It reveals our readiness for the deeper and greater.

TRANSFORMATION THOUGHT

God desires to release an increase of revelation in your life. Recognize what it looks like and position yourself to receive.

REFLECTION QUESTIONS

1. Based on the three methods of recognizing revelation mentioned, list three moments/experiences where you clearly recall receiving revelation from God.

    a. _____

    _____

    b. _____

    _____

    c. _____

    _____

2. What does "stewarding" revelation look like to you? Why do you think stewarding what you have already received positions you for increase?

_____

_____

_____

_____

TRANSFORMATION PRAYER

Holy Spirit, help me to recognize those moments where You are releasing revelation to me. I steward what I have already received, and position myself for increase by obeying what You have already revealed.

ADDITIONAL RESOURCES

Hearing from God
http://store.ibethel.org/p39/hearing-from-god

REVELATION SETS THE BOUNDARY LINES FOR YOUR FAITH

*So then faith comes by hearing, and hearing
by the word of God* (ROMANS 10:17).

Revelation is not for some extremely gifted or special people; it's available to all believers. All of us have been given the great privilege of being able to hear the Word of God. We recognize that the supreme revelation of the Word was given to us in the form of Jesus Christ, and then printed in the form of sacred Scripture. At the same time, Romans 10:17 brings another dimension to this process. We need to move beyond this idea that faith comes simply be reading the Bible and memorizing certain verses. This is helpful, but not the be all, end all of what Paul is saying here.

In the original Greek language, Paul is saying this—faith comes by hearing (*akoē*: instruction, namely *oral*) and hearing by the *rhēma* of God. A key definition of the word *rhēma* is "that which is or has been uttered by the *living voice*." As believers, faith comes by studying Scripture, but also by hearing the *living voice* of God. This is the nature of revelation. It takes realities we may pass over multiple times in Scripture, and places a divine, living emphasis on them.

Why is hearing the *living voice of God* essential for walking in faith and living a supernatural lifestyle? Your faith cannot go beyond what you have been exposed to in revelation. Revelation sets the boundary lines for what you believe. I can read Bible verses day after day about God's healing power, or see examples in the Gospels where Jesus healed the sick, cleansed the lepers, and raised the dead, but if those truths remains words on a page, and if the testimonies remain ancient stories, I am going to live in such a way *today* that is detached from what happened *then*.

We were never designed to approach Scripture this way. Paul reminds us that we have received the Holy Spirit, and He is the Author of all revelation. He notes that the *"letter kills, but the Spirit gives life"* (2 Cor. 3:6). For us to study the Bible without the expectation of hearing the living voice of God, we can easily travel down the road toward intellectualism. We just add to a Bible knowledge base, rather than build our faith to believe for the impossible. Revelation prevents us from taking this route, for it keeps us ever in tune to the living voice that brings three-dimensionality to Scripture. The breath of God is upon its pages, and we begin to see what we had not seen before. The concepts and the stories are relevant for us *today*. Revelation then takes what we see and hear, and uses it to set our boundary lines of belief.

As long as I shun the revelation that God wants everybody to be healed and whole, I have cut myself off from releasing faith in that area. Revelation actually enlarges the arena that our faith can function in.

TRANSFORMATION THOUGHT

Revelation sets our boundary lines of belief. It takes us beyond reading a book or hearing words, and, through the living voice of God, shows us the relevance and prophetic application of the concepts and testimonies in Scripture for our lives today.

REFLECTION QUESTIONS

1. How does revelation set boundary lines for belief? How can it be possible for us to read the Bible, but still place limitations on our faith?

_____

_____

_____

_____

2. Read Romans 10:17 again. What does the reality of the living voice of God mean to you when it comes to reading Scripture and building your faith?

_____

_____

_____

_____

TRANSFORMATION PRAYER

Father, thank You for the gift of Your living voice. I am a son/daughter of God, and Your Word says that I am led by Your Holy Spirit. Continue to open my eyes and ears to receive greater revelation from Your Word so that the boundary lines of my faith are increased and I release greater breakthrough toward the impossibilities of life.

ADDITIONAL RESOURCES

Extreme Living
http://store.ibethel.org/p1169/extreme-living

INCREASING AND EXPANDING REVELATION

Call to Me, and I will answer you, and show you great and mighty things, which you do not know (JEREMIAH 33:3).

Receiving or increasing in revelation is not something we can simply conjure up. We cannot turn it on or turn it off on demand. Increase comes through hunger and pursuit. This passage in Jeremiah is a powerful invitation from God *to us* to actually see His mysteries. The word *mighty* in this context is an Old Testament term for *mystery*. Oftentimes, we assume that divine mystery is out of reach for humanity. Everything unexplained or unanswered tends to get tossed into a file folder called "mystery" and treated as though its contents are inaccessible.

While mystery lives up to its name and does exist beyond the immediate reach of man, we are nevertheless summoned into a quest to hunger for it. God does not hide mystery from us; He hides it for us. The realm of mystery has been made open and available to us! This is one of the roadblocks of thought that must be removed if we are going to experience expanding revelation in our lives. Mystery is *not* off-limits to you.

Remember, revelation sets the boundaries for our beliefs and our faith will not extend beyond these self-imposed boundary lines. If we believe that mystery is off limits and hidden from us, we will not press in for it. On the other hand, if Jesus' words are indeed true and relevant for us today, this sets new boundary lines for how we respond to the realm of mystery. Jesus said, *"it has been given to you to know the mysteries of the kingdom of heaven"* (Matt. 13:11).

It is your level of hunger and desperation that determines the level of increase in revelation that you experience. Picture someone desperate enough to open his or her heart fully and issue a deep cry from the spirit. This is the deep of man crying out for the deep of God. That opening of the heart determines the level of revelation we receive. You are not being summoned into religious works, for they earn us no merit with God. Nor are you trying to convince God to give you something. He has made the realm of mystery available. He is simply looking for those willing to receive the inheritance that has already been purchased and paid for. He is looking for those who are serious and intentional about stewarding what He has provided. I simply can't live life knowing there are realms of mystery, and keys to those realms, that are available to me but which I have not yet discovered. It's not work and toil; it's discovery and access.

Few people I know receive substantial revelations or visitations of God without reckless pursuit. Most people I know who receive revelation cry out day and night for that fullness of the Holy Spirit. Casual prayer gets casual revelation. Deep cries cause God to "hear you" and "answer you" and "show you great and mighty things you do not know."

TRANSFORMATION THOUGHT

The key to experiencing increase and expansion in the revelation you receive is increasing your level of hunger and pursuit.

DISCUSSION QUESTIONS

1. Why do you think people are so quick to assume that mystery is off-limits and out of reach? What does this do to our faith when it comes to actually pursuing and understanding some of these mysteries?

_____

_____

_____

_____

2.   How can you experience increase and expansion in the revelation you receive?

_____

_____

_____

_____

TRANSFORMATION PRAYER

Father, thank You for making Your mysteries accessible to me. Stir up even greater hunger inside of me to access everything You have made available—revelation for me to know You greater, and also revelation that empowers me to more effectively represent You to the world.

ADDITIONAL RESOURCES

The Quest for the Face of God
http://store.ibethel.org/p58/the-quest-for-the-face-of-god

"The Gift of Hunger" 8:30 A.M., June 03, 2012
http://store.ibethel.org/p6371/the-gift-of-hunger-8-30am-june-03-2012

" Jesus was sleeping because He lives in has no storms." Scripture mark 4:35-41

Jesus=God
Prayer (talks) to Jesus (woke Him up)
Jesus prays - sea-"calm" "?"
" How come you don't have any faith?"

Food He said to
Feed them you feed them
+ the word allowed
then to feed the masses.

" to decree enabled."

→Mark 6→
H.S. Revealed
to Jesus that
the disciples were
on the water -
He couldn't see
them that's
how He operated.

Mark 6 → 49 → 52

Math 8 - 17

" All I have seen teaches me
to trust in What I have seen."
con →

BECOME A STUDENT OF THE MIRACULOUS

*We must become students of miracles. That means
the miracles we experience must shape how we think.
Miracles can be dazzling and dramatic, but they
are not primarily designed to dazzle us. God gives
us miracles to train us how to see differently.*

Week Four

VIDEO LISTENING GUIDE

1. Jesus' _____word_____ enabled the food to multiply at the disciples' hands.

2. The same _____decree_____ that multiplied food would also bring the disciples over to the other side of the sea.

3. Exposure to the miraculous challenges us to think _____differently._____

Three Leavens of the Mind

1. Leaven of Herod—_____political_____ and humanistic in nature.

2. Leaven of the Pharisees—Religious mindset, where God is at the center, but He is impersonal and _____powerless_____.

3. Leaven of the _____Kingdom_____ of God.

   - True faith is _____superior_____ to all reasoning. *partners the mind of Christ (perfect intellect)*

   - The leaven of Herod and the Pharisees are both driven by the _____fear_____ of man. *Both driven by the fear of man.*

   - When we can't see or hear what God is doing presently, we _____remember_____ what He did last. *(It's how He works) Remember (prophesy relates to see what He's doing now)*

Day Sixteen

PUTTING REVELATION INTO PRACTICE

*You search the Scriptures, for in them you think you have
eternal life; and these are they which testify of Me* (JOHN 5:39).

This study is structured to help you put revelation into practice. Renewing the mind is not merely reading words on a page and having a moment of insight about a particular verse. That passes for renewal of the mind in many environments and churches, but at best that's only half the equation. Renewal comes as revelation leads you into a new experience with God.

This is exactly what Jesus was talking about in John 5. The religious leaders of His day had access to all of the right information, but it did not produce any type of experience with the Personification of the Scripture who was standing before them. Jesus was and is the ultimate expression of revelation in practice.

We read that in Jesus the Word became flesh and dwelt among us (see John 1:14). Even for God, just providing information was not enough. His people had received centuries of information, all of which was purposed to prepare the way for an experience. If we reject the invitation to the encounter that revelation presents to us, we simply grow in head knowledge. We become more religious. Revelation is intentioned to bring us into a transformative experience with God. The ultimate purpose of a transformed mind is to transform people, who go on to transform cities and nations. It is a process. When we decide to stop at one place in the process, we cease the flow of increase.

When we keep revelation in the form of information, we simply become more religious. This is why you have examples of theologians who read the Scriptures 12 hours a day and have no clue about the Kingdom of God. They can recite endless evidence of their knowledge, but there is nothing revelatory or transforming about their lives.

If we accept the invitation to personal transformation, but never take it to the next level and bring the Kingdom to others, we stagnate. We become a dead sea instead of a river, full of life and vitality. God's will is a steady flow of revelation from His world to this one *through you*. I want you to become revelation with feet, taking what you have experienced and bringing it to a world that is desperate for what you carry (they just don't know it).

When you put a revelation into practice, you won't get it 100 percent right. You might not even get it 50 percent right. But you will learn, and you will grow into a level of maturity you wouldn't otherwise have. The best way we know to learn is to experiment.

TRANSFORMATION THOUGHT

The flow of revelation was never designed to stop with us—whether it is us growing in more head knowledge or even us being transformed; it invites us into a transformative encounter with God that changes us and releases us to transform others.

REFLECTION QUESTIONS

1. How does revelation invite you into an encounter or experience with God? Describe a time where this happened for you. What did it do for your relationship with God?

_____

_____

_____

_____

2.   Why is it so important to protect yourself from just growing in
      information?

_____

_____

_____

_____

TRANSFORMATION PRAYER

*Father, help me to grow in revelation of You by stewarding
what I have already received. Show me how to make this
practical by stepping out, taking risks, and doing the things
You said I am able to do as one filled with Your Spirit.*

ADDITIONAL RESOURCES

The Invasion: Coming Soon to a City Near You
http://store.ibethel.org/p57/the-invasion-coming-soon-to-a-city-near-you

MIRACLES SHAPE THE WAY WE THINK

Miracles actually help us see reality differently. They shape the way we think about what is impossible and possible. If we do not become students of the miraculous, it becomes difficult for us to step out and put revelation into practice. When it comes to putting revelation into practice, we wonder, "What does this even look like?" We try. We fail. We get discouraged. We don't see any immediate fruit. People don't get healed. No instant breakthrough. As a result, we back up from the demands of a supernatural lifestyle, instead of running toward it appropriately.

The key to helping us maintain consistency in pursuing the supernatural life is studying miracles. While they can be dazzling and dramatic, it is necessary for us to receive their invitation. I celebrate the spectacular, but in the same manner, I have learned to celebrate the simple. The one raised from the dead is no more significant than the one who has a crooked bone in the little finger straightened. Naturally, this perspective sounds flawed, because our natural eyes are captivated by what appears more spectacular. The truth is, both expressions of the miraculous are invitations to know the Author of the miracle and discover His ways. This is what supernaturally transforms the way we think.

A miracle is a school. It is a learning opportunity. It is also a nutrient that helps us become stronger, more accurate representatives of God on the earth. It is possible to go through life experiencing a continuous flow of miracles, signs, and wonders, while not extracting what is intended from those experiences. This was undeniably the case with both Israel, in the Old Testament, and even the Pharisees in the New. Both groups were exposed to miracles with regularity, but in both cases, the summons of the miracle was rejected. Both groups refused to accept the invitation and experience transformation that comes only by encountering the God of Miracles.

Miracles happen. We get excited. People think it's really cool. And then what happens? People leave the same way they came. They are thankful for either receiving the miracle or witnessing the miracle, but in the end, they have not learned to see and think differently. They go home and life continues in the same pattern as it did prior to the miracle.

Even the disciples failed the test on occasion. They experienced and even participated in the supernatural multiplying of food in Mark 6:30-44, but then, when faced with the next problem—a stormy, windy sea that they struggled to press through—they demonstrated they had not gotten the message of the previous miracle. They should have recalled their participatory role in the miracle of multiplying the food. If they would have remembered their role in the miracle, they would have responded to the problem of the stormy sea by taking authority over the environmental conditions. Miracles are always a training ground, setting us up to respond appropriately to the next impossibility that we face.

TRANSFORMATION THOUGHT

Miracles are not designed to simply awe and amaze us—God desires that they transform the way we think and approach reality.

REFLECTION QUESTIONS

1. How are past miracles supposed to reshape the way we think and respond to life's impossibilities?

_____

_____

_____

_____

2. In what ways have the miracles you've seen/experienced changed the way you think about God? (How have these miracles impacted your Christian life, even to this day?)

_____

_____

_____

_____

TRANSFORMATION PRAYER

Father, I celebrate Your miracles and wonders. Help me to never just stop at celebrating the supernatural, but use these miracles to transform the way I think, the way I see, and the way I respond to life.

ADDITIONAL RESOURCES

Healing: Our Neglected Birthright
http://store.ibethel.org/p37/healing-our-neglected-birthright

THE LEAVENS OF THE MIND

*Another parable He spoke to them: "The kingdom of heaven
is like leaven, which a woman took and hid in three measures
of meal till it was all leavened"* (MATTHEW 13:33).

The Bible reveals different influences on the mind that determine how we interact with the Kingdom. These influences directly impact our role as students of miracles, and whether or not our minds are actually transformed by encountering the miraculous.

Today, we are going to look at the two forms of spiritual leaven that threaten our appropriate response to the miraculous, thus preventing us from moving forward into a supernatural lifestyle. Jesus told his disciples, *"Take heed, beware of the leaven of the Pharisees and the leaven of Herod"* (Mark 8:15).

The Leaven of Herod

This represents the atheistic influence based on the strength of man and man-based systems. Herod's leaven excludes God completely. The mantra of those under this influence is, "God helps those who help themselves." While this leaven is utterly secular and humanistic, it has nevertheless infiltrated the church creating a form of practical atheism. This influence prevents us from believing in an active, speaking, moving God. This is fleshed out when such believers face situations daily without bringing God into the equation. He exists, but He is detached, disinterested, and unable to really do anything about our circumstances or situations. This leaven creates a culture of unbelieving believers who live exactly like their atheistic neighbors whenever they face a problem.

The Leaven of the Pharisees

This is the influence of the religious system. Such a perspective embraces God in theory, but not in practice or experience. Such a person is drawn to theology, information, and doctrine. All three of these things are good—in fact, vital. However, they are purposed to bring us into a divine encounter, not simply increase our head knowledge, puffing us up. The leaven of the Pharisees exalts knowledge. They have God in form, but without power. They prefer a God they can explain, contain, and control. Even though they assign much of the happenings in the world to "God's sovereignty," this is really the religious mind's way of rejecting the responsibility of a supernatural lifestyle. They also assume an explanation and understanding for everything, exuding a cocky boldness in describing the innumerable problems facing God's people without presenting any solutions.

Both leavens are influenced by the fear of man and motivated by what people think. They offer safe explanations, but no supernatural solutions. Solutions actually offend problems and circumstances, for they insert fresh possibility that problems can change. This challenges the mind, but at the same time, introduces hope that makes way for faith.

TRANSFORMATION THOUGHT

The leaven of Herod tries to keep your mind in the prison of unbelief and skepticism, while the leaven of the Pharisees attempts to keep God as a distant, theological concept.

REFLECTION QUESTIONS

1. How do you see the Leaven of Herod in operation today?

_____

_____

_____

_____

2. In what ways have you personally experienced (or overcome) the Leaven of the Pharisees?

_____

_____

_____

_____

TRANSFORMATION PRAYER

Father, protect my mind from either of these influences. Show me how to live under the continuous influence of Your Kingdom and see that influence release supernatural impact in the world.

ADDITIONAL RESOURCES

Three Leavens of the Mind
http://store.ibethel.org/p176/three-leavens-of-the-mind

THE LEAVEN OF THE KINGDOM

But Jesus, being aware of it, said to them, "Why do you reason because you have no bread? Do you not yet perceive nor understand? Is your heart still hardened? Having eyes, do you not see? And having ears, do you not hear? And do you not remember?" (MARK 8:17-18)

Let's return to the example of the disciples participating in the miraculous food multiplication in Mark 8. Jesus invited them to participate in the miracle, not to dazzle or wow them, but to call them up into a new standard of thinking.

A miracle is a tutor, a gift from God to show us what type of lifestyle exists on the other side. When I experience a miracle and later revert back to the same doubt, complaining, moaning, and groaning, it's because I have not allowed the testimony of the Lord to have its full effect on the way I think. Moving forward after a miracle should recalibrate how we experience life and respond to its problems.

By encountering the miraculous, you are being positioned to maintain the perspective of God in every single trial, circumstance, and situation. What revealed that the disciples flunked their "miracle test"? It was not their participation in the supernatural food-distribution miracle, but rather, it was how they responded in the storm they faced only a few verses later. Our perspective in the aftermath of previous miracles reveals how we allowed the previous miracles to actually reshape our thinking. How we deal with today's problem shows us whether or not we actually received yesterday's invitation to a transformed mind and progression toward maturity.

99

Miracles by themselves do not produce maturity; I agree. But they do carry this seed of unusual potential to produce significant growth and completely redefine how we view and express Christianity. Just seeing a miracle or even receiving a miracle does not guarantee that the leaven of the Kingdom is having its full effect on your mind. We can have eyes that don't see and ears that don't hear in regard to the supernatural.

You and I can be the most Kingdom-minded people on the planet... when things are going well. We can see multitudes healed, dozens saved, have great times of worship. But then I might go home and the car breaks down and suddenly I'm out 3,000 dollars. Then the computer shuts down and the phone system goes out, and the neighbor's mad at me. The fire of circumstance expands whatever leaven is influencing my mind. Let's ensure that, when put to the test, the greater influence in our lives is the leaven of the Kingdom. The key is receiving and responding to the invitation of miracles to upgrade our standard of living so that today's miracle positions us to step into tomorrow's breakthrough.

TRANSFORMATION THOUGHT

The influence of God's Kingdom in our lives is revealed after we see or receive a miracle, as we are getting ready to respond to the next impossible situation we face in life.

REFLECTION QUESTIONS

1. Why is it that our level of Kingdom influence is measured by how we respond after we see or experience a miracle (and not how we behave during a miracle)?

_____

_____

_____

_____

2. How does yesterday's miracle shape and prepare us for today's impossibility? What has this looked like in your life and walk with the Lord?

_____

_____

_____

_____

TRANSFORMATION PRAYER

Father, I pray for an increase of the influence of Your Kingdom in my life. For every miracle that I see and participate in, help me learn the lesson that will prepare me to release breakthrough into the next impossible situation.

IDENTIFY YOUR STORM

And a great windstorm arose... (MARK 4:37).

In the past, we have lumped the concept of "storms" all together. We have assumed that any and every storm we go through is either caused by God, or orchestrated by the devil. The truth is, there are storms the devil causes for our destruction, and then there are storms God orchestrates for our redirection and advancement.

So how do you know what kind of storm you are facing? Is your storm a miracle waiting to happen, like we read about in Mark 4:35-41, or is it a tool that God is using to redirect your path as He did with Jonah? Knowing what type of storm you are in enables you to respond to it correctly. Have you let past miracles "tutor" you to a place of faith adequate for your current challenge? The disciples' storm was sent by the devil to keep them from the will of God. Jonah's storm was sent by God to turn him back to the will of God. Some people face storms because they took a left when God told them to take a right. God brings a storm in His mercy to drive them back on course. Others face storms because they are in the middle of God's will.

Read Mark 4:35-41. Here, we see an example of a storm purposed to steal, kill, and destroy—all hallmarks of the enemy's nature and intentions. Here is what we need to remember. Even though our tendency is to cry out and ask God to intervene in our situation, we need to reconsider the invitation of past miracles. Even if you have never seen or experienced a miracle for yourself, go to the pages of Scripture. The miracles contained in its pages are your invitations to elevate your standard of life today. Remember, God never allows a storm without first providing you with the tools that will calm the storm. While God allows such storms, they are never allowed for the purpose of defeating us, but instead, He wants us to defeat them through the resources He has given us and bring about a miraculous result.

We may feel like the disciples did, as they woke Jesus up and asked, "Don't You care that we're perishing?" While Jesus did end up answering their prayer and calming the storm, He responded with a strange question, *"Why are you so fearful? How is it that you have no faith?"* (Mark 4:40). In this situation, it was their responsibility to command the obstacle to disappear. Most people's concept of ministry involves trying to get God to fix problems on earth when we should be commanding the storms to be calm. We should see situations from Heaven's perspective and declare the word of the Lord over them—and watch Heaven invade.

The storm is your invitation to steward the miracles you have experienced. Let's not waste our miracles. Let's not watch God do something awesome, then give a little golf clap, a little "amen" and walk away unchanged. Let's recognize that we are equipped for every storm. We have been trained by past miracles to release present solutions.

TRANSFORMATION THOUGHT

By identifying the kind of storm you are going through, you are empowered to respond to it correctly.

REFLECTION QUESTIONS

1. How have you seen "storms" in the past? How has God been changing the way that you respond to them in your life?

_____

_____

_____

_____

2. Why is it so important that you know what type of storm you are facing?

_____

_____

_____

_____

TRANSFORMATION PRAYER

Father, I ask for wisdom that shows me what kind of storm I am going through—or what type of storm someone else is going through. Help me to identify the storm and respond correctly so I can either bring breakthrough, change direction, or make the necessary adjustments. Thank You for equipping and empowering me with the tools to get through every single storm that comes my way.

ADDITIONAL RESOURCES

The Perfect Storm
http://store.ibethel.org/p177/the-perfect-storm

HOW TO BELIEVE IN YOUR OWN SALVATION

"Remember that Jesus addressed believers as saints. We tend to think sainthood is acquired after years of sacrificial service. Wrong. We went from rotten sinners to born-again saints in a single moment when we accepted salvation. Once the blood of Jesus has wiped out sin, you can't get any cleaner."

- Heb. 11:11 Sarah believe me...
- Once the blood of Jesus us covers something
  It is illegal to bring it out again.

Romans 8:39. , Corith.
   things present or things to come.

- Jesus called Peter a rock long before he
  deserved the title –

With no sore eyes eyes see the fear + call it
   out + address it.   Eph 2:10

You are being masterpiece of Gods grace.

  Everyone stops to make gods

not our faith in humanity but our faith in the blood
           of Christ.

     Luke 4:1-13 – 1st temptation brought to
              Jesus was identity.

1 I Adam – temptation in the garden was to ? what
                    God said.

Prays tools enemy uses ① ?. what God has said
                  ② what god wants who you are.

God Almighty called us + thats how
            we got saved – called us to life + we
stop bring up old issues said yes.
      up for re-evaluation.

Saying yes to Jesus no longer need to be
      reevaluated.

Week Five

VIDEO LISTENING GUIDE

8 Keys to Fully Believing in Your Salvation

1. At salvation, you didn't lose the ability to sin; you lost the ability to _enjoy_ sin.

2. As you are in Christ, the Father looks at you like He looks at _Jesus_.

3. When God records your story in His account, He only records what took place after _Repentance -_.

4. To revisit the past apart from the blood of Jesus is to open oneself up to a spirit of _deception_. _because you are opening yourself up to something that no longer exist_

5. Your past can separate you from your _awareness_ of _a lie._ the love of God.

6. God both forgives sin and removes the _nature_ from which sin came. _Remove the entire root of stem - changes who you are @ the core of your being._

7. When we see people as forgiven and as saints, we treat them _different._ _So speak to the inward gift of God - That which is born in a person to obey God._

8. The enemy frequently addresses the lie of _identity._

Keys to Being Anchored in Your Identity

1. We _settle_ into what God has said.

2. Get identity from _who_ called us. _Significance delike I am is not where we get our idty._

~ Always the people of God as people identy. who have a nature to obey God. ~

LIVING IN AGREEMENT WITH OUR INHERITANCE

I pray that the eyes of your heart may be enlightened,
so that you will know what is the hope of His calling,
what are the riches of the glory of His inheritance
in the saints (EPHESIANS 1:18 NASB).

Believers have received an absolutely priceless inheritance in Christ. This is what provoked the apostle Paul to intentionally pray for the eyes of our hearts to be enlightened so that our mortal minds—through the renewing work of the Holy Spirit—could grasp the inheritance we have received in Christ.

I strongly believe that many Christians eat cheese and crackers, in spiritual terms, when our "fare" bought us a full banquet. When our minds are not in complete agreement with the inheritance we received at salvation, we will continue to live beneath our potential in God. The key word is *agreement*. This is not a call to understand everything that the blood of Jesus made available at Calvary. We will be living in constant surprise and amazement to what God released through His Son's sacrifice throughout all eternity. He is forever the worthy Lamb.

Understanding follows agreement, and agreement is another word for belief or faith. Previously, we spoke about the boundary lines of belief that cause us to either extend our faith for something or not. The subject we are discussing this week is an absolutely foundational boundary line of belief. If we do not get this down, we will continue to live defeated and powerless, when in fact, every provision has been made for us to live from a position of secured, assured victory in Christ.

When we talk about a lifestyle of miracles and what it looks like to walk in the supernatural, many believers have a difficult time stepping into this inheritance. This is because they fail to grasp the magnitude of their salvation. We deal with thoughts of unworthiness when our minds are not convinced that we really are guilt-, sin-, and shame-free because of the blood of Jesus.

Too often Christians live under the influence of yesterday's failures, blemishes, and mistakes. When we do, we depart from the normal Christian lifestyle and live under the influence of a lie. Needless to say, this lie halts the renewing of our minds and keeps us from living in the "everyday miraculous" that should be normal for every born-again believer.

TRANSFORMATION THOUGHT

Believers live beneath their inheritance when they see their failures and mistakes as greater than the redemptive work of Christ. It is a correct understanding of salvation that grants us access to a supernatural life of miracles.

REFLECTION QUESTIONS

1. How is it possible for a believer to live below his or her inheritance? What does this look like?

_____

_____

_____

_____

2. What are some practical ways that you can remind yourself of your inheritance in Christ?

_____

_____

_____

_____

TRANSFORMATION PRAYER

Lord, help me to live fully aware of every blessing and provision You made available because of the Cross. Show me how to access this inheritance, not live beneath it.

ADDITIONAL RESOURCES

It Is Finished
http://store.ibethel.org/p1735/it-is-finished

Day Twenty-Two

BREAKING FREE FROM THE UNWORTHINESS DECEPTION

And you, who once were alienated and enemies in your mind
by wicked works, yet now He has reconciled in the body of
His flesh through death, to present you holy, and blameless,
and above reproach in His sight (COLOSSIANS 1:21-22).

We have this idea that by focusing on and emphasizing our unworthiness, we are being more humble. If we spend our Christian lives fixated on our unworthiness, we are doing two things: For one, we are believing a half-truth, which is a lie, and second, we become paralyzed from moving forward and advancing the Kingdom.

A half-truth is no less than a full lie. This concept of unworthiness needs to be confronted, because if we continue to believe we are unworthy, then we will never position ourselves to receive from God. After all, *we are unworthy.* This is no longer a condition, but an identity. Yes, none of us through our own merits or works is worthy to receive anything from God. This is absolutely true. However, in His grace, God looked upon you as worthy of the greatest gift conceivable—the life of His precious Son.

Jesus is the One who makes us worthy. Any worthiness that we have received is not our own, but belongs entirely to Christ Jesus. He is the one who qualified us to become worthy, or holy, in the Father's sight. To embrace a present identity of unworthiness is the ultimate expression of living beneath the inheritance of salvation. Salvation actually changed our identity entirely. We became new creations who were worthy to come before a holy God, not because of our works, but because of Jesus' work.

This open door is available, and yet so many deny this invitation because they remain under the deception of unworthiness.

This leads us right into the second problem that this deception of unworthiness causes—restricted Kingdom advancement. We never position ourselves to step out and bring Heaven to earth because we consider ourselves unworthy of such a task, and unfit to receive the tools He has made available—His presence, His power, His gifs, and His supernatural ability. Unworthiness puts us under the delusion that in order to demonstrate the Kingdom, perfection is required. The apostles prove that such is not the case. Yes, a pursuit of maturity and integrity and character development is part of the package. This is not license for us to exclusively pursue the power and tools of God while neglecting realities such as discipleship, maturity, and character formation. Jesus never gave an either/or option. It was not some "pursue the miracles" at the expense of character situation, or vice versa. Purity and power are cornerstones of the supernatural life. Perfection, however, was only achieved by one Man, and that Perfection is what authorizes us—faults, problems, growth processes and all—to walk out the supernatural life as normal Christianity.

Living under yesterday's condemnation doesn't make us more humble. If anything, it keeps us focused on ourselves instead of on the Lord. It's much more difficult to humbly receive forgiveness we don't deserve than to walk in false humility, cloaked in yesterday's shame. When we receive free forgiveness, the One who gave it to us is honored. When He is honored, we are truly humbled.

TRANSFORMATION THOUGHT

Believing that we are unworthy before God is not humility; it is a sign that our thinking is out of alignment with what God did for us through the Cross.

REFLECTION QUESTIONS

1. Why do people think that believing they are "unworthy" is a sign of spirituality or humility? What does this deception actually do to our ability to receive from God?

_____

_____

_____

_____

2. How do you currently see yourself? Do you believe it is in alignment with how God sees you?

_____

_____

_____

_____

TRANSFORMATION PRAYER

Father, help me to see myself like You see me. I am worthy. I am clean. I am forgiven. I am your son/daughter. I have been adopted into Your family. Jesus' blood made me worthy to receive all access to Your Presence. Help me to live out of this glorious inheritance all the days of my life!

ADDITIONAL RESOURCES

What It Means to Be Forgiven
http://store.ibethel.org/p60/what-it-means-to-be-forgiven

SETTLE THE IDENTITY QUESTION

*For we are God's masterpiece. He has created us
anew in Christ Jesus, so we can do the good things he
planned for us long ago* (EPHESIANS 2:10 NLT).

It's difficult, if not impossible to demonstrate the will of God "on earth as in Heaven" if we don't think of ourselves as truly forgiven, and if we hang on to a false view of our identity. Deception about identity effectively cancels out most of our potential in ministry. Some people reduce each day to, "I hope I survive" instead of, "What will God do today through me?" This has everything to do with how we see ourselves in light of our new identity in Christ. We have been created anew in Christ Jesus. Heaven sees us as *God's masterpiece.* If this is how God sees you, you must begin to see yourself the same way.

Paul connects the concepts of recognizing identity and doing the works of the Kingdom. If we do not believe that we are God's masterpiece, we will not step out and begin to do the *"good works which God predestined (planned beforehand)"* (AMP). The supernatural exploits of the Kingdom are not reserved for the perfect; they are prepared for those who recognize and agree with their identity in Christ.

When we succumb to guilt and shame, we give in to the single oldest temptation in the Bible—the temptation to question our identity and God's identity. This is right where the enemy wants to keep us—as those who live unsure of their identity in Christ and thus remain unable to step out and perform the works of the Kingdom that push back darkness. The serpent has been working at this deception for a long, long time.

The very first temptation in the Bible was not to partake of forbidden fruit, but to question what God had said. The serpent said, *"Has God indeed said, 'You shall not eat of every tree of the garden'?"* (Gen. 3:1). Once he got them to doubt God's integrity and identity, it was easy to lure them into foolish actions. In the same way, before the devil tempted Jesus with anything else, he tried to pry Him away from His identity: *"If You are the Son of God..."* (Matt. 4:6). He wanted Jesus to doubt His identity—so what is the devil's strategy with you and me? *The same thing!*

We are the people God loves, the people God forgives. We are the House of God, the gate of heaven on earth. When Moses asked God, *"Who am I that I should go to Pharaoh, and that I should bring the children of Israel out of Egypt?"* (Exod. 3:11), God appeared to ignore the question by answering, *"I will certainly be with you"* (Exod. 3:12). But that was the answer! Moses said, "Who am I?" God said, in effect, "You are the man God goes with." Who are you, brother or sister? You are the person God hangs around with. You are clean and forgiven. That is your identity!

TRANSFORMATION THOUGHT

In order to accomplish the supernatural exploits that God has prepared we must believe that we are exactly who He says we are.

REFLECTION QUESTIONS

1. How does questioning our identity as God's masterpiece hold us back from accomplishing the things we have been called to do?

_____

_____

_____

_____

2. What are some practical things you do/can do to remind yourself of who God says that you are (your identity in Christ)?

a. _____

_____

b. _____

_____

c. _____

_____

d. _____

_____

e. _____

_____

f. _____

_____

g. _____

_____

h. _____

_____

TRANSFORMATION PRAYER

Holy Spirit, I ask You to remind me of how the Father thinks about me. May His thoughts shape the way I think about myself and live my life. Help me to be settled in what He thinks about me and not allow my mind to be swayed by any false ideas about my identity.

ADDITIONAL RESOURCES

Grace? ...Hell Yes!
http://shop.ibethel.org/products/grace-hell-yes

"Jesus Is Our Model" 8:30 A.M., December 20, 2009
http://store.ibethel.org/p3323/jesus-is-our-model
-8-30am-december-20-2009

Day Twenty-Four

DEAD TO SIN, ALIVE IN CHRIST

*Even so consider yourselves to be dead to sin, but alive
to God in Christ Jesus* (Romans 6:11 NASB).

As your mind continues to be renewed and you discover your identity in
Christ, it is key that you believe you are actually dead to sin and alive
in Christ. The unworthiness deception produces people who label themselves by who they were, not who they have been remade as in Christ.
But even consider this: Before you were brought into the Kingdom of
God, there was still significance on your life. Even though we are sinners
by nature, God still loves, values, and pursues us. Paul makes this evident
when he describes how *God demonstrates His own love toward us, in that
while we were still sinners, Christ died for us* (Rom. 5:8).

There is no grey area when it comes to what we think about our
nature. We either believe that we are dead to sin, and alive in Christ
(according to Romans 6), or we believe that we are still sinners by identity.

Are you washed in the blood of Jesus? Then you need to think of
yourself as dead to sin and alive to Christ. This is your new, redeemed
nature. It's not a mind-over-matter thing, but has everything to do with
the power of supernatural thinking. It involves you awakening to what's
been real and true since the moment you met Jesus: As a born-again fol-
lower of Christ, you are dead to sin.

More than just quoting a Bible verse, we need to live as though this
supernatural reality is true—because it is. The blood of Jesus was completely sufficient to transform your identity. Prior to Christ, sinning was
what you did. It was normal and natural, because you sinned by nature.
It could be done without a second guess. Now, things have shifted. There

is a reason that, even when we do miss it and sin, it feels unnatural. This is not an invitation into condemnation, as many of us embrace it to be. The unnatural feeling accompanying sinful behavior reminds us that we are no longer sinners by trade. Such sinful thinking or actions are actually uncomfortable for us now. They are atypical.

When a believer sins, he or she is not behaving out of nature. The believer is doing something that is entirely unnatural, as he or she is now redeemed. The Holy Spirit has transformed your nature completely. Sin no longer comes out of who you are, but out of what has been left behind. Even though your spirit is reborn when you give your life to Christ, your soul and flesh take a lifetime to catch up. It is a progressive journey of maturity, growth, renewal, and development. This is the process of sanctification.

In short, sanctification is bringing every other area of your life into alignment with what took place in your spirit at conversion. Your very identity—the core of who you are in your spirit—was miraculously transformed when you were born again. The old was gone and the new had come.

TRANSFORMATION THOUGHT

When you are saved, your identity changes from a sinner to a saint; you no longer sin by nature because you are no longer a sinner by identity.

REFLECTION QUESTIONS

1. What is the danger of thinking that, when we sin, we are still sinners by nature?

_____

_____

_____

_____

2. Why do you think you experience an "unnatural feeling" when you sin? How should this be encouraging instead of condemning?

_____

_____

_____

_____

TRANSFORMATION PRAYER

Father, thank You for supernaturally transforming my nature. I am no longer a sinner; I am a saint, cleansed by the blood of Jesus. His blood made me a new creation. I am dead to sin and alive to God in Jesus Christ.

ADDITIONAL RESOURCES

Transformed People Transform Cities
http://store.ibethel.org/p4771/transformed-people-transform-cities

Or you can get the first message in the above series:

"Transformed Series: Really Saved" 11:00 A.M., June 27, 2010
http://store.ibethel.org/p3924/transformed-series-really
-saved-11-00am-june-27-2010

YOU ARE COMPLETELY FORGIVEN

*Therefore, if anyone is in Christ, he is a new
creation; old things have passed away; behold, all
things have become new* (2 CORINTHIANS 5:17).

The death of Christ completely wiped out your record of sin. This may seem like grammar school teaching, but most people do not live with the realization that they are totally forgiven. They can quote the Bible verses, but they don't live under the influence of their truth. The blood of Jesus wiped out the power and record of sin in your life. Your old nature is dead. It hasn't been put on a shelf, or in a closed room, or imprisoned—it has been crucified. Period. Done deal.

In Christ's death, your nature died along with Him. In His resurrection, you were raised with Him. Continuing in this context, Paul writes that "*Now if we died with Christ, we believe that we shall also live with Him*" (Rom. 6:8). We cannot move quickly past this Scripture, otherwise, we miss the truth that can completely revolutionize the way we walk out our salvation. Too many believers live in restraint because they are not convinced of their complete forgiveness. Our minds must embrace the reality that *we died with Christ*. If our nature died with Christ, it is dead. On the flip side, when we were raised with Christ, we became entirely new creations. It is like a new species emerged from the grave. Old things have passed away, according to Second Corinthians 5:17. Paul did not add that *some* things have become new, implying that there are some sins beyond the reach of Jesus' blood. If we are in Christ, *all* things have become new, meaning that we are completely forgiven and live as sons and daughters of God who bear a completely new nature.

Consider it. When the enemy tries to bring up a sin from your past, he is talking about something non-existent. It's completely legal for you to say, "I didn't do that. The person who did that is dead. *This* person has never done that." Either the blood of Jesus is completely effective, or it's not effective at all. And it does not just wipe away the punishment so that when you die you don't go to hell; rather, the blood of Jesus has the power to completely transform us into a new creation in Christ. This radically transforms the way we live on earth and represent Jesus to the world around us.

It is amazing how mindfulness of past sin can actually separate us from our awareness of present identity. This is why it is so important for us to have the forgiveness issue completely settled in our hearts. We need to move forward in the revelation that we are totally forgiven.

TRANSFORMATION THOUGHT

Because of Jesus' blood, our past has been released and our sin has been completely forgiven. Our old nature was buried with Christ, and we were raised with Christ as completely new creations.

REFLECTION QUESTIONS

1. How does it change the way you see your salvation when you actually believe that you are totally forgiven of sin?

_____

_____

_____

_____

2. What does it mean to you that just as your old nature was buried with Christ in His death, you were raised with Him through His resurrection?

_____

_____

TRANSFORMATION PRAYER

Father, help me to live like I am completely forgiven of sin. My old life was buried with Christ and because of His resurrection, I am a new creation. I am a new species of person with a completely new nature. The old is gone, and the new has come. Show me how to live mindful of the new nature I received because of Jesus' resurrection!

ADDITIONAL RESOURCES

"The Art of Living Clean" 8:30 A.M., August 12, 2012
http://store.ibethel.org/p6526/the-art-of-living-clean
-8-30am-august-12-2012

THE POWER OF REMEMBERING

One of the great tools for keeping a Kingdom mindset is to meditate on and remember God's Word, devising ways of reminding ourselves of His promises to us, and then passing those promises and remembrances on to the next generation of believers.

I will never
loose from my curriculum
the supernatural power of God.

The gospel to reminisce
what God has done.

Psalm 78 9-11
They tempted God they limited God —
They didn't remember His
power.

I refuse to project the
awareness that God
invades the impossible.

The testing of Jesus is the spirit
of prophecy — (The
anatomy of the prophets)

VIDEO LISTENING GUIDE

1. When the supernatural invasions of God become removed from our _Conversation_, we expect them even less.

2. Supernatural interaction with God maintains our _Courage_ to obey during difficulty and impossibility.

3. If you do not walk in a lifestyle of radical obedience, you become _Cowardly_ in conflict.

4. When you lose awareness of the God who invades the impossible, you will start thinking too _Small_. — You are un restrit to what God wants you to do in a

5. When we stop living conscious of the God who invades the _certain_ impossible, we begin to reduce _minisry_ to our gifts. situation

6. Be _accurate_ when you share testimony.

Benefits of Testimony

1. The _Culture_ of testimony creates an environment where the invasions of God are continuous and ongoing.

2. If you remain conscious of what God has done in the past, it will empower you to be _Confident_ in a present circumstance.

testmny Has the ability to chnge the present

— Be acurate don't embelish Your testmny

Any story where Jesus gets the credit

AN INVITATION TO MEDITATION

I will also meditate on all Your work,
and talk of Your deeds (PSALM 77:12).

A vital key to remembering the works and Word of God—and experiencing their transformational impact on our minds—is practicing biblical meditation.

Before moving on, I want to make it clear that there is a difference between Eastern meditation and biblical meditation. Just because a counterfeit version of something exists does not give us license to throw out the entire practice. Abandoning biblical meditation has been very costly to the body of Christ. By lumping all versions of meditation together, and throwing out the authentic version, we have stopped short of experiencing the renewal of the mind Paul writes about in Romans 12.

We are able to memorize different Bible verses and quote them at seemingly appropriate times—and yes, we experience a measure of breakthrough here. But God is inviting us into a lifestyle, not an isolated experience. I celebrate every miracle, all the while recognizing that each one is an invitation to pursue a lifestyle where miracles are normative, not the exception.

To walk in the miraculous with the degree of regularity that is available, we need to step beyond memorization and enter the realm of meditation. Eastern meditation demands that its adherents empty their minds. This is incredibly dangerous, for it makes one susceptible to deception and demonic infiltration.

Biblical meditation, on the other hand, involves filling our minds with God's truth. Do you see the difference? The counterfeit version empties the mind, while biblical meditation fills the mind with truth. By filling our minds, we subject ourselves to the transformative power of God's Word. By making this form of meditation our pursuit, we fill our minds with something living, eternal, and supernatural. Living Truth produces transformation. Memorization is one thing, but when we commit to filling our minds with the Word of God, feeding upon it as necessary food, our thought life collides with God's glory, and His glory and presence are released through encountering His Word.

Paul shows us in Second Corinthians what happens when any part of our lives is brought into a collision with glory—we *are being transformed into the same image from glory to glory, just as by the Spirit of the Lord"* (2 Cor. 3:18). Meditation advances this process of transformation in the mind, conforming your very thinking into the image of Christ, so that you start thinking *like* Him.

TRANSFORMATION THOUGHT

Biblical meditation involves filling our minds with God's transformative truth.

REFLECTION QUESTIONS

1. What have you thought about biblical meditation in the past?

_____

_____

_____

_____

2. What do you think it looks like to fill your mind with God's truth? List any practices you currently use that help you do this.

_____

_____

_____

_____

TRANSFORMATION PRAYER

Father, show me how to fill my mind with Your truth. Thank You that as my mind encounters Your Living Word, it is transformed to reflect the mind and thoughts of Christ.

ADDITIONAL RESOURCES

Filled with the Fullness of God

http://store.ibethel.org/p36/filled-with-the-fullness-of-god

SHIFTING WORRY TO MEDITATION

You will keep in perfect peace all who trust in you, all
whose thoughts are fixed on you! (ISAIAH 26:3 NLT)

I want to follow up yesterday's topic by equipping you with some practical ways you can biblically meditate. This is not a practice that is reserved for an elite, super-spiritual few. The good news is if you can worry, you can also meditate. In fact, worry is the counterfeit of meditation. Same principle; wrong emphasis.

The problem is that many people are more skilled at worrying than they are meditating, when in fact, we all possess the capacity to go either way. I want to help you choose the road less traveled—biblical meditation.

Every person, saint and sinner alike, meditates every day. The question is, what are you meditating on? Here is an example. Say you've got a problem with your finances. A person with a renewed mind derives joy even in that circumstance because joy comes not by what is seen but by what God says. This person practices biblical meditation, filling his or her mind with the promises of God. In turn, they are not only able to quote a Bible verse at their problem, but their entire thought process is transformed to reflect the way God thinks about their situation. They go from a fear or worry perspective to a provision perspective. They know that God is not a liar and He will keep His word.

The problem is, there is a little voice called worry that steals in and reasons with you, saying, "Years ago you disobeyed the Lord financially, and now you will reap what you sowed." That might sound like a pretty good argument, and it might cause you to shift your meditation from

God's Word to worry. We empower what we agree with. If we start making mental agreement with this deceptive argument, it becomes a more consuming thought process and it begins to replace our provision perspective. Soon that little voice has grown so big it's like a megaphone in your ear, drowning out the truth of God's perspective.

The voice that drowns out *every* other in your mind should not be worry or fear; it should be the steadfast, unchanging Word of the Lord. Instead of recalling God's abundant promises of provision, we choose to give ear to the enemy and focus on the lie he is introducing into our thought process.

It is essential that when thoughts counter to God's Word come against us, we follow Isaiah 26:3 and keep our minds *fixed* upon the Lord. We need to make ourselves inconvincible. This happens through the process of biblical meditation.

TRANSFORMATION THOUGHT

The secret to maintaining God's perspective when dealing with trials or circumstances is keeping our minds fixed upon His truth. We cannot allow fear or worry to convince us to second-guess God's promises.

REFLECTION QUESTIONS

1. What does it look like to keep your mind "fixed" upon the Lord according to Isaiah 26:3?

    _____

    _____

    _____

    _____

2. Write down three things you can start practicing that will help keep your mind fixed upon God and His truth.

    a. _____

    _____

b. _____
   _____

c. _____
   _____

TRANSFORMATION PRAYER

Father, help me to keep my mind fixed upon You—even in the midst of storms, trials, and circumstances. Empower me not to be swayed or convinced by thoughts that are in disagreement with Your truth. I stand, by the power of the Holy Spirit, convinced that what You said is steadfast and true.

ADDITIONAL RESOURCES

"Faith When Answers Are Delayed" 6:00 P.M., May 20, 2012
http://store.ibethel.org/p6322/faith-when-answers-are-delayed
-6-00pm-may-20-2012

WRITE IT DOWN!

Write the vision and make it plain on tablets, that
he may run who reads it (HABAKKUK 2:2).

Writing down what God has done in the past empowers you to run with faith in the present. Perhaps you have been encouraged to journal many times before. I know it can be one of those cumbersome tasks that we feel obligated to do, and ultimately becomes easy to neglect.

One of the main things that prevents us from faithfully recording what God has done—either in a journal, or writing things down in a computer document, or posting them on sticky notes, or jotting them on note cards—is a lack of motivation caused by an absence of vision. Vision is what actually encourages us to keep a written record of God's acts. We need a vision for why we are doing what we are doing. If we don't see the purpose for diligently recording the miracles and works of God, we will not be motivated to do it. Our lack of vision will cause us to give up on the task easily. However, when you have a clear understanding of *why* you keep track of what God has done in your life, I can assure you, it will be your joy and delight to record everything He does in whatever format makes the most sense to you.

We maintain written records of God's acts and miracles because it empowers us to remember His faithfulness—even when we are having difficulty bringing His faithfulness to mind by ourselves. There are times when we are facing certain struggles or impossibilities that, for whatever reason, it is like our minds become completely blank and blinded. We are fortunate if we are able to recall the goodness of God in saving our souls and bringing us into the Kingdom to begin with! Why? Worry comes in like a flood. It is worry, fear, and the sheer gravity of what we are currently facing that distract us from focusing on God's faithfulness. This is typical. This is why there was such a strong emphasis placed on the need to maintain written records of God's exploits, particularly throughout the Old Testament. These records were passed on from generation to generation, keeping the stories of God's miracles alive for all to experience and press into as their own.

This is why I personally keep a written record of what God has done. I keep a journal for my children and my grandchildren that they might see what God did in my lifetime. We even have a staff member at our church whose entire job description is to record the miracles that happen in and through our church and with our ministry teams. I want people to know the great and mighty works of the Lord long after we're gone, so they can run with the vision even further.

TRANSFORMATION THOUGHT

Keeping a written record of God's acts and miracles is a vital reference point for us, reminding us of God's faithfulness. If He performed the miraculous in the past, He will surely move again, for He does not change.

REFLECTION QUESTIONS

1. How have you attempted to keep written records of what God has done in your life?

_____

_____

_____

_____

2.   Why is it important for you to keep a written record of God's miracles in your life?

_____

_____

_____

_____

TRANSFORMATION PRAYER

Thank You, Father, for every miracle You have performed in my life. I commit to remembering these mighty acts. Strengthen me to follow through keeping a written record of Your works, not as a duty or religious exercise, but as a way to constantly remind myself of Your faithfulness in my life.

ADDITIONAL RESOURCES

The Power of the Testimony
http://store.ibethel.org/p46/the-power-of-the-testimony

REVIEW WHAT GOD HAS DONE

If you should say in your heart, "These nations are greater than I; how can I dispossess them?"— you shall not be afraid of them, but you shall remember well what the Lord your God did to Pharaoh and to all Egypt (Deuteronomy 7:17-18).

Once we write down what God has done, we are then encouraged to review it. A written record is no good unless we go back and review what we wrote down. To simply fill journals and notepads up without ever returning to them is pointless; however, when we go back and review what God has done for us, we become strengthened. When our minds consistently remember what God did in the past, we position our lives to walk in present victory.

In Deuteronomy 7, God was encouraging His people not to be afraid of the nations they were being called to dispossess. Even though these nations appeared to be great and mighty people, God invited Israel to review what He had done in the past. Past victory positions us to demonstrate present faith. Reviewing what God has done postures our hearts to believe that the same God who moved yesterday will *move again*. The key to Israel's courage and strength was remembering how God moved in Egypt.

During the Exodus, Egypt was undeniably a world superpower. And yet, God miraculously redeemed His people out of slavery using a shepherd and a staff. The key is training our minds to remember rather than immediately react. Our natural reaction to impossible situations and circumstances is one of "How am *I* going to make it through this?" The fault in this perspective is that it is completely wrapped up in us. God knows this. He is fully aware of every possible line of thought our minds entertain when coming up against the impossible.

This is exactly why He gave Israel words of encouragement like Deuteronomy 7:17-18. He is calling our imagination to come up higher. By recalling what God has done, we force our imaginations to become Kingdom imaginations. The testimony of what the Lord has done helps us to remember who God is, what His covenant is like, and who He intends to be in our lives. Every testimony of His work in someone's life is a prophecy for those with ears to hear. It is a promise that He'll do the same for us because God is no respecter of persons (see Acts 10:34) and He is the same yesterday, today, and forever (see Heb. 13:8). By reviewing what God has done, we feed on His faithfulness according to Psalm 37:3.

Even if you do not have any journals or past writings of what God has done in your life, simply return to the Bible. This passage in Deuteronomy is one among many divine invitations to remember the record of God's mighty acts in the lives of His people.

TRANSFORMATION THOUGHT

Reviewing the past history of God's acts—in our lives and in the lives of His people throughout history—strengthens us to walk in present-day faith.

REFLECTION QUESTIONS

1. In what ways do you currently review what God has done in your life? How does this remind you of His faithfulness and give you strength to face today's challenges?

_____

_____

_____

_____

2. How does this concept of reviewing what God has done help you see and apply the Bible differently?

_____

_____

_____

_____

TRANSFORMATION PRAYER

God, I celebrate the great things You have done, both in my life and throughout history! You have a track record of consistent faithfulness because You are faithful. You were faithful to Your people throughout Scripture, and You remain faithful today. Thank You for being unchanging. If you moved mightily in the past, You will do it again—and bring great glory to the Name of Jesus!

ADDITIONAL RESOURCES

Recovering Our Spiritual Inheritance
http://store.ibethel.org/p48/recovering-our-spiritual-inheritance

REMIND GOD OF HIS WORD

"Remember Abraham, Isaac, and Israel, Your servants, to whom You swore by Your own self, and said to them, 'I will multiply your descendants as the stars of heaven; and all this land that I have spoken of I give to your descendants, and they shall inherit it forever.'" So the Lord relented from the harm which He said He would do to His people (EXODUS 32:13-14).

Moses is reminding God of the promise He swore to Abraham. This is not because God is forgetful. To remind God of His Word is an indicator that we have written down what He has done, reviewed it, and now we are responding. Reminding God is the action step in the process of remembering.

In Exodus 32, God was angry with the Israelites because they were worshiping the golden calf as Moses was up on the mountain with Him (see vv. 7-10). In fact, God went as far to say that He was going to wipe out all of His people and start over through Moses, making a nation out of him! (See Exodus 32:10.) It was obvious that, somehow, Moses had kept a record of what God had promised in the past to Israel's forefathers. Clearly, he remembered and reviewed what God had said to and done for His people hundreds of years prior to this moment.

After God proposed to destroy His people, Moses reminded God of the multigenerational promise He made to Abraham, Isaac, and Israel. As a result of Moses' intercession, God did not end up harming His people. Here we see how the principle of reminding God is the action step in the remembering process we have been studying during this session.

THE SUPERNATURAL POWER OF A TRANSFORMED MIND

The principle of reminding God of His Word truly carries over from the Old to New Testament, passing through the Cross.

Reminding God has nothing to do with us helping out His divine memory. He does not need any assistance from man. When we remind God, we demonstrate that our minds have been supernaturally shaped by His past works and promises. We remember what He has done. We mediate on these things. We write them down. We review them. And finally, we remind God of who He is, what He has done, and what He has said. Reminding God is the fruit of a transformed mind. His miracles didn't merely dazzle us and His promises were not simply Bible verses we spoke aloud when dealing with a difficult situation. Our minds have been so impacted by what He has said and done, we think differently—so much so that when we experience situations that are in disagreement with God's will, we bring them before Him and remind Him of His supernatural solutions.

TRANSFORMATION THOUGHT

Reminding God of His past miracles and promises is our action step in the remembering process. It reveals that our minds have been transformed by what He has done and what He has said.

REFLECTION QUESTIONS

1. What does this process of reminding God of His Word look like to you?

_____

_____

_____

_____

2.   Why do you think it is important for us to first record what God
     has done for us and review these things in order to accurately re-
     mind God of His promises?

_____

_____

_____

_____

TRANSFORMATION PRAYER

Thank You, Father, for continuing to change the way I think. Help me to remind You of past promises and miracles when I deal with circumstances in my life today. May Your words and works so deeply and so powerfully shape the way I think that when situations come up that are not Your will and do not reflect Your character, I come before You and remind You of the divine solution You have prepared for the problem I am facing.

ADDITIONAL RESOURCES

Prayer: The Kind that Changes the World
http://store.ibethel.org/p47/prayer-the-kind-that-changes-the-world

Not on My Shift: Praying in the New Day
http://store.ibethel.org/p44/not-on-my-shift-praying-in-the-new-day

ENDURING UNCERTAINTY

"One of the toughest lessons a Christian can learn is how to trust and praise God in the uncertain time between a promise and its fulfillment. I believe it is a powerful act of spiritual warfare to stand in the middle of death and disease, conflict and unresolved issues, and to cause your spirit to rise and give thanks to God."

Mark 11:11 - 17

Jesus makes comparison bet. His
ministry + John the Baptist ministry (old
test. ministry - "hopeless" represented
in the Law related to sin + uncleanness.)
We only knew sin & to it was
contagious. sin is severe.
But new testament - Shift - spotless
Lamb - Righteousness is contagious.

Living in regret make
Your deepest regret.

VIDEO LISTENING GUIDE

1. We cannot reduce the will of God to what we have ___Seen___ happen.

2. If you feed yourself on what God has done, and is doing, you can always stay ___Encouraged.___ .

3. ___Offense___ with God leads to unbelief and resistance to the purposes of God. Math 11:6.

4. We cannot afford to think about our present or future ___differently___ than God does.

Keys to Navigating Through Disappointment

1. Keep ___Promises___ before us constantly.

2. ___Celebrate___ God's goodness through praise.

KEEP YOUR THEOLOGY CONSISTENT WITH GOD'S CHARACTER

Jesus Christ is the same yesterday, today, and forever (HEBREWS 13:8).

For I am the Lord, I do not change (MALACHI 3:6).

The great temptation for us during times of uncertainty is to adjust our theology to agree with the circumstance, rather than keeping it in agreement with the written record of who God is. By keeping our focus on what Scripture says about who God is and who Jesus revealed Him to be, we are given anchors that sustain us in the seasons between promise-received and promise-fulfilled. The key is, we cannot allow our theology to bow to our circumstances.

This is not a call to deny reality. In order to see our circumstances transformed and come into agreement with God's Kingdom reality, we must confront them *as they are*. The disease. The brokenness. The hurt. The pain. The need. We must honestly acknowledge what needs to be transformed in order to measure it beside the revealed will of God. We have the Scriptures and we have the example of Jesus Christ. Either one cannot be trumped by our experience or theology. Theology and experience are derived from the Word of God. This is the foundational starting point.

In order to endure uncertainty, we need to build on that which is certain. Jesus is certain. The rock of His Word is certain. The nature and character of God is certain. It is absolutely vital that we identify these certainties so we can be sustained in times of tension. Again, tension exists when there is a promise in God's Word that is yet unfulfilled. Tension exists until the gap no longer exists, and what was promised comes to pass. However, tension makes faith necessary.

Fulfillment does not demand faith. When we receive what God promised, faith is no longer necessary—at least faith for that specific miracle. One day, when we behold Jesus with our eyes in all of His glory, faith will no longer be necessary. What we believed in faith, on earth, will become a visible reality. In the meantime, faith must be in something sure and certain, otherwise, it will shift based on our circumstance. If we are experiencing sickness—and we are not receiving instant healing—it is easy to conclude that God is not Healer. Likewise, if we are believing for financial provision and it seems like nothing is happening, despite how much we pray, there is the tendency to conclude that God is not coming through.

We make conclusions like this when we do not know how to stand firm in seasons of uncertainty. What keeps us grounded in faith? The truth that our God is unchanging. Jesus Christ is the same yesterday, today, and forever!

TRANSFORMATION THOUGHT

When we experience seasons of uncertainty—the gap between receiving a promise from God and seeing that promise come to pass—we must remain grounded in the solid, unchanging truth of who God is. His character is eternally unchanging, even though our circumstances change.

REFLECTION QUESTIONS

1. What does it mean to keep our theology rooted and grounded in who God is, rather than letting our circumstances dictate what we believe?

_____

_____

_____

_____

2. How does Scripture and the example of Jesus show us who God is and what He is like? How can you make these your "anchors" in times of uncertainty?

_____

_____

_____

_____

TRANSFORMATION PRAYER

Jesus Christ is the same yesterday, today, and forever. Father, You are unchanging. Show me how to base my faith on who You are instead of what my circumstance is saying. Regardless of what I am up against or go through in life, I choose to believe You are exactly who You say You are, and who the Word reveals You to be.

ADDITIONAL RESOURCES

"It Is All About Jesus" 11:00 A.M., July 19, 2009
http://store.ibethel.org/p2773/it-is-all-about-jesus-11-00am-july-19-2009

Day Thirty-Two

RECOGNIZE THE POWER OF YOUR PRAISE

But you shall call your walls Salvation, and
your gates Praise (ISAIAH 60:18).

Praise sustains and develops us in the midst of uncertainty. It keeps us focused on what is eternal. It is our response to the unchanging, consistent nature of God. We offer God thanks for what He does, but praise is a response to His nature and character—His eternal attributes.

In Revelation 21:21, we see this gate again and learn that it is made out of solid pearl. How are pearls formed in an oyster? Through irritation and conflict. A granule of sand gets inside an oyster shell, and a pearl forms around the granule to keep it from doing harm. The Bible's pairing of praise with irritation is not coincidental. When we are stuck in conflict and uncertainty, and yet we praise Him without manipulation, it is a sacrifice. We are not merely praising God to get something out of Him, or using it as a formula in hopes of simply adjusting our circumstances. We know who He is. We are grounded in the fact that He is faithful. In praise, we are responding to what we know and what we are sure of concerning the unchanging character of God.

Just as irritation produces a pearl in the oyster, something beautiful is formed in us as we praise God in the midst of uncertainty. Praise forms a gate—a place of entry where the King of Glory can come in and invade our situation.

Praise responds to God for who He is. This allows us to keep our situations and circumstances in appropriate perspective. Remember, we are not denying the reality of our problems; however, we are denying them a place of emphasis. What will our point of focus be? If it is

God, then we will surely praise, for such is the only fitting response to beholding Him.

If our focus is our problem, we position ourselves to experience the theology adjustment we studied about yesterday. When our problems are in greater focus than God, our theology about God is reshaped according to the problem. However, when our focus upon the Lord is greater than our problem, our theology dictates the level of influence that the problem has over our lives.

Even in uncertainty, we can deny our problems that place of influence over our lives. Praise is what maintains this perspective. When God is magnified in our sight, everything else comes into proper focus.

TRANSFORMATION THOUGHT

Praise is our response to the unchanging character and nature of God. It reveals that we are anchored in the midst of uncertainty, that we know who God is, and even builds and matures us through the process.

REFLECTION QUESTIONS

1. In what ways can praising God build you up while you are going through a time of uncertainty?

_____

_____

_____

_____

2. Write down some obvious character traits that you can praise God for right now—especially if you are currently going through a season of uncertainty, while waiting for one of His promises to come to pass.

a. _____

_____

b. _____
_____

c. _____
_____

d. _____
_____

e. _____
_____

TRANSFORMATION PRAYER

I will bless You at all times, Lord. Your praise shall continually be in my mouth! You are my steadfast anchor through every season. Your Word is eternally true. Even though situations and circumstances change, You are the Lord who does not change. I praise You for everything You are!

ADDITIONAL RESOURCES

Changing Your World
http://store.ibethel.org/p32/changing-your-world

Day Thirty-Three

KEEP YOURSELF ACCUSATION-FREE

The thief does not come except to steal, and to kill, and
to destroy. I have come that they may have life, and that
they may have it more abundantly (John 10:10).

One thing that some Christians do when they find themselves in a place of uncertainty, with no answer for their problem, is change their view of God. As a result, they ascribe to Him character traits that are totally anti-biblical. We accuse Him of sending the circumstance rather than going to His Word and allowing our minds to be transformed based on His eternal perspective of our problem.

Uncertainty causes some people to misunderstand who God is. They begin to deny God's true nature and embrace sickness and disease, poverty and mental anguish as gifts from God. That is a devastating lie from hell because we are accusing God of actually doing the work of the enemy.

The reason people do this is because they want answers so badly during times of uncertainty that they invent theological answers to make themselves feel good about their present condition. Even though our present condition, in and of itself, does not feel good—be it a sickness, broken relationship, financial hardship, loss of a job, addiction, or bondage—we desperately want to come up with a reason behind it. We mistakenly assume that because it's not changing, there must be some divine purpose to it. This is especially true when after our first, second, or third prayer attempt it looks like nothing is shifting in the natural. The boulder is still there. Rather than going to the Source and defining the situation based on what God says, it is more appeasing to the natural mind to sacrifice the truth about God on the altar of human reasoning. This is the exact opposite of what the renewed mind produces in us.

When our minds are renewed, we embrace what God says and what God thinks, regardless of what the circumstance says. When our minds are bent toward a more natural, earthly perspective, we allow the circumstance to dictate to us who God is and what His will is. Just because the situation does not immediately change, the natural mind concludes that the problem is God's will. As a result, we come up with different reasons why God is permitting the problem, or, even worse, reasons why He sent the problem to begin with. This is falsely accusing Him of works that are contrary to His very nature.

Two things are happening here. One, circumstances are not changing; instead, our minds are being changed by the circumstance. Two, our view of God is not impacting the circumstance, but rather, our view of God is adjusted according to the state of our circumstance.

Let's define this clearly: God is good all of the time. The devil is bad all of the time. We do ourselves a tremendous service to remember the difference between the two. Healing, salvation, wholeness, provision, and joy have already been given to us. They can't be recalled or returned. They are facts of Kingdom living. They were paid for by Jesus on the Cross.

TRANSFORMATION THOUGHT

When our circumstances do not immediately change and we endure seasons of uncertainty, we are tempted to redefine who God is based on our situation. We then start accusing Him of actually sending problems into our lives that are contrary to His very nature and character.

REFLECTION QUESTIONS

1. Why do you think it is so important to biblically determine what God is like versus what the devil is like?

_____

_____

_____

_____

2. How can you protect your mind from accusing God and redefining who He is during seasons of uncertainty and waiting?

_____

_____

_____

TRANSFORMATION PRAYER

You are good. You are the Author of abundant life. I recognize that the thief came to steal, kill, and destroy, but Jesus came so that I would walk in abundant, supernatural life. Help me to know Your character so that I can recognize when You are at work and also see when the enemy is at work. Protect me from an accusation mentality by keeping me grounded in Your goodness.

ADDITIONAL RESOURCES

Enduring Faith
http://store.ibethel.org/p35/enduring-faith

Day Thirty-Four

PROTECT YOUR MIND FROM OFFENSE

For we walk by faith, not by sight (2 CORINTHIANS 5:7).

In addition to accusing God for sending problems our way, it is also easy for our minds to become intellectually offended with God because of what we have not seen come to pass.

Many times I hear people say things like, "I wish I could believe God heals people today, but my grandmother died two weeks ago and we prayed for her and she didn't get healed." Or, "I wish I could believe that God loves me, but I just went through a horrible divorce, and I know a good God wouldn't allow that kind of pain." Heartfelt, genuine grief separates people from God because they have questions, but no answers.

One of the key tools to protecting our minds from this type of offense is through walking by faith, not sight (see 2 Cor. 5:7). I repeat, this is not embracing some false mentality that nothing bad ever happens in life when we exercise faith, or that by simply praying in faith, everything will magically change in that very instant. Paul did not encourage us to simply speak by faith or pray by faith; he intentionally told the church in Corinth to *walk* by faith. This implies an entire way of living.

The Message Bible phrases Paul's statement in Second Corinthians 5:7 this way: *"It's what we trust in but don't yet see that keeps us going."* Offense with God is birthed when our focus becomes fixated on the things we have not seen come to pass yet, and we assume that because they did not instantly materialize when we prayed, they will not be answered. Faith in the unchanging nature of God and the eternal steadfastness of His promises keeps us steady when we are living between the unseen and seen. We trust in promises that remain unseen, believing they will break into the seen

171

realm. However, just because the answers and solutions promised by God's Word are unseen right now, this does not mean they are any less real than the circumstances we presently see with natural eyes. Again, offense comes when we treat the unseen with a natural mind instead of a renewed mind.

A renewed mind does not step out and redefine God's nature based on promises that have not been fulfilled yet. Rather, the renewed mind is aware that unseen promises are just as real as the circumstances we see with our natural eyes. Sometimes, we think that just because we do not see our miracle come to pass immediately, the miracle remains non-existent. The raw materials for every miracle and breakthrough already exist in the realm of Heaven. We know Heaven is real, even though we cannot presently see it with our eyes. If Heaven is real, then everything in Heaven is also real. I invite you to see the unseen from a renewed mind, as this will protect you from offense.

Remember, all of God's promises in Christ are *Yes and Amen* (see 2 Cor. 1:20). We don't need to convince Him to deliver on what He said; He already has!

TRANSFORMATION THOUGHT

A renewed mind recognizes that all of God's promises are "Yes and Amen" in Christ; this sustains us through periods of uncertainty, reminding us that every promise—although unseen—is just as real as the circumstances we presently see. We do not define God based on our changeable, visible problems, but rather upon unseen eternal truth.

REFLECTION QUESTIONS

1. How can you protect your mind from becoming offended with God?

_____

_____

_____

_____

2. What does the reality of "walk by faith, not by sight" look like to you? How can it keep you safe from an offended mind?

_____

_____

_____

_____

TRANSFORMATION PRAYER

Father, I will not become offended with You. I thank You that even in times of confusion, You welcome my questions. Protect our communion, Holy Spirit. As I walk by faith, I ask You to keep me from being distracted by false ideas about who You are.

ADDITIONAL RESOURCES

How to Overcome Disappointment
http://store.ibethel.org/p311/how-to-overcome-disappointment

PRESS THROUGH WITH PERSEVERANCE

Then He (Jesus) put His hands on his eyes again
and made him look up. And he was restored
and saw everyone clearly (Mark 8:25).

If Jesus had to pray for a blind man more than once for him to receive healing, we should also recognize the need for perseverance when it comes to enduring uncertainty. Too many give up the fight and come into agreement with their circumstances instead of persevering for a promise.

This is where accusation and offense set in. We accuse God of giving us the problem and theologically conclude that He allowed it or gave it to us for some divine purpose. This is false. Likewise, we become offended with God because we perceive that nothing is happening or giving way in the situation. This is also a wrong perspective for us to embrace. Uncertainty demands persistence and perseverance. If Jesus needed to pray again for someone's complete breakthrough and healing, we need to follow His model.

When we find ourselves in those uncertain seasons of life, we are like the disciples in their moment of failure—where they prayed for a demonized boy, but nothing happened (see Mark 9:28-29). They were the most miracle-experienced people on earth at that time. No one had seen more and done more than they, and yet they came up against something for which they could get no solution. This is still true today. We may find ourselves facing problems and not knowing where the tools are to bring about the solution. But that doesn't mean the problem is insurmountable. There is power in resolving in your heart that God is good all of the time, and that His will for healing and wholeness does not change, despite what we see in the natural.

This is what fuels your attitude of perseverance. The opposite is giving up and concluding that, "Just because we could not set the boy free from demonic torment, it was not God's will for him to be delivered at all." This is how some respond today when immediate results do not come in response to their prayers or risks of faith.

How do we endure uncertainty, resisting the temptation to accuse God or become offended with Him? Persevere. Press on. Persist. We are only able to persevere to the extent that we are intimately acquainted with God's character. His nature backs up His promises. When we know that the One who promised is also faithful, it does not matter what opposition, resistance, or uncertainty comes against us. We cling to the anchor of truth that the God who promised is also faithful to bring His promises to pass.

TRANSFORMATION THOUGHT

It is essential for us to persevere and persist to experience the promises of God; by giving up, we consent to the circumstance and deny ourselves the potential of a breakthrough.

REFLECTION QUESTIONS

1. How can perseverance and persistence be classified as essential tools for warfare when dealing with circumstances in life?

_____

_____

_____

_____

2. Recall a testimony where you prayed for something/someone and, rather than happening instantly, the miracle came through perseverance. Why was it important than you did not give up, even during those times of uncertainty?

_____

_____

_____

_____

TRANSFORMATION PRAYER

God, You are faithful. Just as You are faithful, Your promises and Your Word are faithful. I cling to them in every situation for they sustain me. They sustain me in uncertainty. They sustain me through questions. They sustain me through waiting. Your goodness empowers me to keep persevering and persisting until Your promises come to pass.

DREAMING WITH GOD

"Absolute surrender to the will of God is the only way for the believer to live. Yet something strange happens as that person enters into the intimacy of friendship with God; God becomes interested in our desires. And ultimately, He wants our minds renewed so that our will can be done."

Psalm 37:4.

God disciplines us because
He wants our will to
be done~
Partnership!!!

Psalm 115:16 — Heart of God.

Prov 13:12

John 14:12-15
15:4,5
"Fruit"

Tree of life stepping into
our Eternal
purpose.

Desires fulfilled
not in repent
God but because of God.

John 16:24
Joy may be
made full.

A balanced life is not scale
between Joy + depression!
Live Full & Joy!!

Desires fulfilled is the Tree of life.

God is looking for a people who dream!

Week Eight

Those things God is drawing you into your purpose = dream! Mark→
— What you dream —
11-23-24

VIDEO LISTENING GUIDE

1. God makes Himself ___vulnerable___ to the desires of His people. He is a relational god. Not looking for contracts.

2. The Lord wants to unveil His purposes in the earth through the dreams and desires of His ___people.___

3. Often we crucify the ___reserected___ man in the name of discipleship.

4. The inside of the Kingdom is ___bigger___ than the outside.

5. Creativity is needed in the place of ___influence.___

6. God will always say "no" to whatever ___undermines___ our purpose. God protects the destiny of every single purpose

7. Much of the church is waiting for the next command from the Lord; He is waiting to hear the ___dreams___ of His people.

8. Pay attention to the desires that come up as you are in God's ___presence.___

Reserection life!

Prov. 8 —
God + the person
GW is done
The 1st creative.

Adam had a role in the nature of the world he was going to live in!

181

YOU ARE A CO-LABORER WITH GOD

For we are labourers together with God
(1 CORINTHIANS 3:9 KJV).

The transformed mind frees you to be one positioned to work together with God, where your will and your desires actually release His purposes into the earth.

However, many Christians have a one-dimensional perspective of this idea of co-laboring. They think it's a robotic interplay between themselves and God in which their will is dialed down to zero and His will completely overtakes their desires and thoughts. They see themselves as remote control beings, totally under the direction of a God who sits in Heaven and works the master controls. But that is exactly the opposite of what the Bible says.

Paul's language in First Corinthians 3:9, and then later on in Second Corinthians 6:1, points to a different reality, where you and I have the joy of working *together with Him*. In fact, your ideas and desires and dreams have a monumental influence on how God carries out His plan in the world. Remember, all of us have been handcrafted in the image and likeness of God.

It is a mistake for us to pray and ask God, "Let me decrease as You increase." I am not second-guessing the good intentions that motivate this request. The problem is we have taken a correct statement and have assigned it incorrect context. John the Baptist made the statement, "*He must increase, but I must decrease,*" (John 3:30) when his public ministry was coming to a conclusion, and it was time for Jesus' ministry to take off. Even John the Baptist's statement does not suggest what many think it says, which is, "God, take all of my humanity and completely overthrow it with Your will." In pursuing this complete overhaul of our will, we are neglecting the collaboration with God that produces a people whose own free will and desires are actually celebrated by God. We know this because of how God created man in the Garden. God's works reveal His intentions, and when He fashioned humanity, He made men and women with a free will. What a pleasure for the Father to watch those who, by choice, worship Him through their own dreams and desires.

When God re-created you at salvation, He did not throw out your humanity. He did not sacrifice your uniqueness. Your uniqueness brings Him glory. Remember, we are co-laborers, meaning that apart from Christ our work is not complete, and at the same time, amazingly, His work on earth is not complete without us. Even though He could accomplish everything and anything He needed to on the earth in less than an instant, God intentionally looks to you and me as contributors to what He is doing, not just robots carrying out His ideas. He actually is interested in your desires and dreams and has opened up His plan on this planet to your influence. Amazing.

TRANSFORMATION THOUGHT

When God created humanity, He did not make robots; instead, He made people with free will who, through their own dreams and desires, could actually worship God by choice and collaborate with Him to fulfill His purposes on the earth.

REFLECTION QUESTIONS

1. What do you think about this truth that God has opened up His plans to your influence? What does this mean to you?

_____

_____

_____

_____

2. How do you think God receives glory through your dreams and desires coming to pass?

_____

_____

_____

_____

REFLECTION PRAYER

Thank You, Father, for this incredible invitation to co-labor with You. Show me what it means that You actually celebrate my desires. My plans. My creativity. Thank You for creating me in Your image and likeness to display Your glory by being the unique person You have made me to be.

ADDITIONAL RESOURCES

"The Land of Promises" 6:00 P.M., December 29, 2013
http://store.ibethel.org/p8111/the-land-of-promises
-6-00pm-december-29-2013

FRIENDS COLLABORATE WITH FRIENDS

*No longer do I call you servants, for a servant does
not know what his master is doing; but I have called
you friends, for all things that I heard from My
Father I have made known to you* (JOHN 15:15).

Abraham and Moses are called friends of God. The result of these collaborative, intimate relationships is absolutely stunning, for Scripture shows us two men who actually had influence with God. This influence is not some right to tell God what to do. Intimacy does not seek to control; it is all about sharing and exchange. What we see extended to both Moses and Abraham is an invitation into the Holy One's decision-making process. Both examples show us how co-laboring with God works.

James tells us that *"Abraham believed God, and it was accounted to him for righteousness.' And he was called the friend of God"* (James 2:23). When God was looking to destroy the wicked cities of Sodom and Gomorrah, it was Abraham He invited into the decision-making process. Based on what we observe from their discussion, it would appear that Abraham possessed a significant voice of influence before God. God had a very clear plan—bring total destruction to these wicked cities. However, Abraham recognized that his nephew, Lot, was living down there. This is what compelled him to intercede for the cities. God is God. He could have done whatever He wanted. The moment He made up His mind to destroy Sodom and Gomorrah, He could have gone right on out and done it. But in this example, God made a choice to show Abraham, and generations to come, what friendship and collaboration with Him looked like.

In Exodus 33:11, we read that *"the Lord spoke to Moses face to face, as a man speaks to his friend."* What is a common denominator of friendship with God? Access into His divine decision-making process and yes, influence in the process. This is demonstrated with Moses after the golden calf incident. Moses had been up on the mountain with God for a while, the people became restless, and ultimately, they decided to worship a golden calf as the "god" who brought them out of Egypt. As a result, God invites Moses into His plan: *"Now therefore, let Me alone, that My wrath may burn hot against them and I may consume them. And I will make of you a great nation"* (Exod. 32:10). How does Moses respond? He invites God to remember the covenant He made with his forefathers, which promised, *"I will multiply your descendants as the stars of heaven; and all this land that I have spoken of I give to your descendants, and they shall inherit it forever"* (Exod. 32:13). In this case, we see that Moses steps into his identity as a friend of God, dialoguing with God about His intentions and actually reminding Him of the covenant that He established with Abraham, Isaac, and Jacob. The result of this interaction? God relents from harming His people (v. 14).

Both of these conversations took place between intimates, not servant and master. Jesus affirmed that we have this kind of relationship with God in John 15:15. Servants aren't co-laborers; friends are. There are major differences between the mentalities of each. A servant is task-oriented, wanting to know exactly what is required so he or she can do it. But a servant doesn't know the master's business from the inside. This is the grace of friendship—*access* to the mind and heart of the Master.

TRANSFORMATION THOUGHT

God has brought you into an intimate, collaborative relationship with Himself where you are invited into His decision-making process, awarded exclusive access into what He is doing, and are also given a voice of influence before His throne.

REFLECTION QUESTIONS

1.   How do you think God gives His people a voice of influence today in His decision-making process?

   _____

   _____

   _____

   _____

2.   Why do you think friendship and intimacy with God is so important in the process of collaborating with God?

   _____

   _____

   _____

   _____

TRANSFORMATION PRAYER

What a joy to be called Your friend! Thank You, Jesus, for inviting me into the greatest relationship of all. You no longer call us just servants, for servants don't know what the Master is doing. You invite Your people into close, intimate friendship. You call me Your friend, and this means that You share Your heart, Your plans, and Your decisions with me.

ADDITIONAL RESOURCES

Friendship with God
http://store.ibethel.org/p27/friendship-with-god

"The Blank Check" 11:00 A.M., September 18, 2011
http://store.ibethel.org/p5427/the-blank-check-11-00am-september-18-2011

Day Thirty-Eight

YOU ARE FREE TO DESIRE

Hope deferred makes the heart sick, but when the
desire comes, it is a tree of life (PROVERBS 13:12).

Your desires, far from being evil, are intended to make you strong and healthy in all areas of life. Desire is, by nature, of the Father. But before we come to Christ, our desires are corrupted because desire springs from what we commune with. This truth is very important, especially in the context of friendship with God.

If we commune with greed, our desires will be greedy. If we commune with pornography, our desires will be for perversity. If we commune with anger over a past hurt, our desire will be for revenge. But when we commune with the Father, our desires are pure. Communion shapes our desires to express the character of our object of communion. We discovered this while reviewing the invitation into friendship with God. Living in His presence and enjoying this friendship with Him awakens us to pure desire.

Sometimes we think that if we really desire something, it must not be of God. It's as if we serve a barbaric God who wants to wipe out anything that springs from our own hearts.

On the contrary, God is enamored by your desires. He wants to see what makes you tick. Yes, He made you and knows everything about you, but He can only commune and engage with you as you open yourself up in relationship with Him. That's where true pleasure is derived, when dreams and desires spark dialogue and interaction with God, and the co-laboring begins.

In Proverbs 13:12, the Bible calls the fulfillment of your desires a tree of life. We can partake of the fruit of this tree in our everyday lives at this present time. God has figuratively placed this tree within our reach, and every bite of its fruit releases in us strength and eternal courage, a sense of destiny and purpose. Where does that tree spring from? From the fulfillment of our individual, unique, God-given desires. Desire is part of God's system, His economy. He draws us into intimate friendship with Him, then responds to our desires and prayers, and answers them. When He does, it releases the courage of Heaven into us.

Many steer clear of desiring anything from God, concerned that their dream or desire may not be in agreement with God's will. His will is not for you to live cowering before Him, afraid to tell Him what you dream or desire. If it is not His will for you, He will not condemn you. Remember, if He cancels one, it's only because He's got a better one in mind!

TRANSFORMATION THOUGHT

God is not against your desires. When your desires are fulfilled, they become a source of life-giving nourishment and strength for you.

REFLECTION QUESTIONS

1. Why do you think people tend to be concerned about their desires not being from God? Where do you think this perspective comes from?

_____

_____

_____

_____

2. How are you strengthened and encouraged when your desires are fulfilled? In what way does reflecting upon past fulfilled desires become a source of courage for you today?

_____

_____

_____

_____

TRANSFORMATION PRAYER

Father, You delight in my desires coming to pass. I don't dream or desire independent of You; I am shaped by Your Presence. I share my dreams and desires openly with You, Father, because You celebrate them and they reveal You!

ADDITIONAL RESOURCES

Dreaming with God
http://store.ibethel.org/p34/dreaming-with-god

Day Thirty-Nine

SUPERNATURAL CREATIVITY IS RELEASED

*Then God said, "Let Us make man in Our image,
according to Our likeness"* (GENESIS 1:26).

You were made in the image and likeness of *the* Creator. Though the planet is filled with those who dream, build, create, and imagine, the very spirit of the creative process involves people functioning in their divine design. God created mankind to model Him, and one of the most clear ways we do this is through the creative process.

So often we assume that to "create" for God involves waiting for some massive download from Heaven. It is like we are expecting to hear God audibly tell us what the lyrics should be, or how the script should develop, or what twists and turns there should be in the novel, or what color the house will be in the painting, or whatever. We mistakenly assume that if we do not wait for either the audible voice or internal witness of the Holy Spirit giving us specific clarity on what direction to take in the creative process, *we are missing God.*

You are wired to create. Yes, there are undeniably times when the Holy Spirit comes upon us strong and we begin to create *out of the Presence.* There is an unusual grace to write, to build, to imagine, to sketch, to draw, etc. Some call this inspiration. When we are hit with it, the creative process flows seamlessly. However, these moments of inspiration tend to be the exception, not the norm. And yet, the act of creating through our free will is just as much an act of worship as it is when we create because of a divine flow of inspirational grace and presence. One way or the other, creation is taking place and the invisible God is being made visible through a people behaving in His likeness.

Dreaming with God unlocks the deep reservoirs of creativity in each and every person, in different areas of gifting and talent. But in too many sectors of the Church, creativity is on lockdown because people fear their desires and dreams. The problem is we have reduced what the expressions of glory and worship look like by placing restraints upon creativity. We assume that creativity is only godly when it is being expressed in a religious setting. This is simply not true. If anything, it is those who would never set foot into a religious meeting who need to behold the image of the Creator *most*.

Religion, cruel and boring, bottles up the creative impulse God has put inside of every person. Each of us has a right and responsibility to express ourselves creatively in whatever area of life interests us.

TRANSFORMATION THOUGHT

When we create, we are modeling God. This is not limited to a religious setting or spiritual context; when we create according to the gifts and talents we have been divinely wired with, we are giving visible expression of the Creator to the world.

REFLECTION QUESTIONS

1. In what ways has God wired you to be creative?

    a. _____

    _____

    b. _____

    _____

    c. _____

    _____

    d. _____

    _____

e. _____

_____

2. When you use these gifts and talents, how does it makes God visible to the world (beyond just being confined to a religious setting)?

_____

_____

_____

_____

TRANSFORMATION PRAYER

Father, I celebrate all of the gifts, talents, and creative abilities You have given me. (Take this opportunity to specifically list some of these gifts and talents that come to mind.)

Holy Spirit, show me and show Your people what it looks like to arise, shine, and release Your light in the earth by modeling You through being creative.

Day Forty

THE DIVINE YES

For all the promises of God in Him are Yes, and in Him
Amen, to the glory of God through us (2 CORINTHIANS 1:20).

The lifestyle that follows a transformed mind is one that says "Amen" to everything God has said "Yes" to in the Person of Jesus Christ. This is why we have been studying different aspects and dimensions to what renewing the mind looks like.

Again, it is not just memorizing a Bible verse or having scriptural facts ready to pray over a specific situation. There are people who use these formulas, but end up seeing very little sustainable fruit in their lives because, soon enough after they experience one victory, another impossibility comes their way. Repetition and even memorization do not set us up for a sustained, supernatural lifestyle. This only comes when our minds undergo a continuous transformation process, where the very thoughts of God permeate our thoughts. We *live* mindful of every single promise that Jesus personified when He walked the planet. This is why Jesus is the *divine Yes*. Everything He said and did while living on the earth shows us what God says "Yes" to, thus revealing the most complete picture of God in all of history. Jesus Christ is, Himself, perfect theology. Anything you think you know about God that you can't find in the person of Jesus, you have reason to question.

This is why keys like friendship, intimacy, and collaborating with God are so important. It is not simply knowing a formula or a principle, but about enjoying friendship with a Person. Paul makes it clear to us that the promises of God are in *Him*. They are not in the principles; they are in the Person of Jesus Christ. We cannot spend our lives pursuing principles, all the while never knowing the One these very principles reveal. The problem for those who become motivated by principles is they are often driven by personal benefit, not relationship.

We want user-friendly principles to appropriate the promises of God so that we can experience the results we read about in Scripture. The desire to see Kingdom results and fruit is completely healthy, but results should always be the result of intimacy, not in exchange for it. Fruit is produced by those who abide in the vine (see John 15:5). It is through this process of abiding that we become so deeply and intimately acquainted with the Word of God through the Person of Jesus, that we are authorized to ask for *what you desire*, and then actually expect *what you desire* to come to pass (see John 15:5-8).

When your desires are fulfilled they become a tree of life to you. The tree of life provides continuous emotional strength, financial strength, wisdom, a mind that's at ease. That is God's desire for you and for every believer.

TRANSFORMATION PRAYER

Father, I ask You to give me a greater, clearer glimpse of You. Help me to think about You differently—that every thought I have in my mind would be a thought that was in Your mind first.

ANSWER KEY

SESSION 1: HOW TO THINK FROM HEAVEN'S PERSPECTIVE

1. Repentance
2. Shift
3. Impossible
4. Heart
5. Enhances
6. Representation
7. Empower
8. Possession

Keys to Thinking from Heaven's Perspective

1. God
2. Answers

SESSION 2: YOUR MIND, GOD'S DWELLING PLACE

1. Experience
2. Restrict
3. Cooperates
4. Lie
5. Empower
6. Worlds
7. Fulfillment
8. World
9. Options

SESSION 5: HOW TO BELIEVE IN YOUR OWN SALVATION

1. Enjoy

2. Jesus

3. Repentance

4. Deception

5. Awareness

6. Nature

7. Differently

8. Identity

Keys to Being Anchored in Your Identity

1. Settle

2. Who

SESSION 6: THE POWER OF REMEMBERING

1. Conversation

2. Courage

3. Cowardly

4. Small

5. Ministry

6. Accurate

Benefits of Testimony

1. Culture

2. Confident

SESSION 7: ENDURING UNCERTAINTY

1. Seen

2. Encouraged

3. Offense

4. Differently

Keys to Navigating Through Disappointment

1. Promises

2. Celebrate

SESSION 8: DREAMING WITH GOD

1. Vulnerable

2. People

3. Resurrected

4. Bigger

5. Influence

6. Undermines

7. Dreams

8. Presence

LOOKING FOR MORE FROM BILL JOHNSON AND BETHEL CHURCH?

Purchase additional resources—CDs, DVDs, digital downloads, music—from Bill Johnson and the Bethel team at the online Bethel store.

Visit www.bjm.org for more information on Bill Johnson, to view his speaking itinerary, or to look into additional teaching resources.

To order Bethel Church resources, visit http://store.ibethel.org.

Subscribe to Bethel.TV to access the latest sermons, worship sets, and conferences from Bethel Church.

To subscribe, visit www.bethel.tv.

Become part of a Supernatural Culture that is transforming the world and *apply* for the Bethel School of Supernatural Ministry

For more information, visit www.ibethel.org/school-of-ministry.